BEDOUIN JEWELLERY IN SAUDI ARABIA

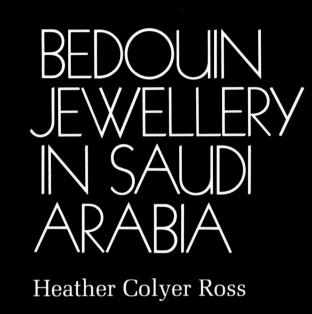

BEDOUIN JEWELLERY IN SAUDI ARABIA

Heather Colyer Ross

Previous page: This enormous qiladah, *or necklace, is old but the components are still in good order. This is due to the thickness of the silver and the content of base metal in the alloy. The embellishment on the pendant and beads is engraving and chasing. The beads are of a lower silver content than the pendant. It is not unusual for beads and pendants on the same necklace to differ in decoration or quality of silver so this threading may be original. The domes of these beads and the pendant bells were raised by the embossing technique. Actual size depicted.*

Bedouin Jewellery in Saudi Arabia
New and revised edition published by
Arabesque Commercial SA
P.O. Box 9
1815 Clarens–Montreux
Switzerland in 1996
First published by Stacey International in 1978

© 1978 and © 1989 Heather Colyer Ross

© 1996 revised edition

ISBN 2 88373 002.4

Library of Congress Cataloguing-in-Publication Data

Ross, Heather Colyer, 1936–
    Bedouin jewellery in Saudi Arabia/Heather Colyer Ross. – 1st U.S. ed.
        p. cm.
    Previously published: 2nd ed. London: Stacey International, 1978.
    Includes bibliographical references and index
    ISBN 0–88734–655–3 (alk. paper)
    1. Bedouins–Jewelry–Saudi Arabia. 2nd. Ethnic jewelry–Saudi Arabia. I. Title.
NK7373.6.S2R67 1995   95–32178
739.27'09538–dc20   CIP

Design: Anthony Nelthorpe MSIAD
Assisted by: Paul Draper
Indexer: Michele Clarke
Maps: DP Press, Sevenoaks
Illustrator: Michael Hadlow, DP Press

Typeset in Melior
by DP Press Limited, Sevenoaks, England
Printed and bound by Royal Smeets Offset, Weert, The Netherlands

The photographs of the author's collection of Bedouin jewellery were taken by Heather Colyer Ross, who also took the photograph on page 118 of the painting by Malin Basil.

The publishers are grateful to the authors and publishers of the books listed in the bibliography for permission to quote from them.

CONTENTS

Author's note

"It is seventeen years since this book was first published, and I am delighted to see that it remains popular. Although I am still pleased with the appearance of **Bedouin Jewellery in Saudi Arabia**, it is time to revise the contents. I take this opportunity to give readers the benefit of additional information that I have gathered.

The collection of Bedouin silver jewellery on which this book is based is the result of the combined efforts of my husband and myself since 1969. Most of the pieces were bought in the Women's *Suq* in the capital city of Saudi Arabia, Riyadh. Initially, my aim in producing a book about this jewellery was to provide something enjoyable as well as informative and, if the book does bring pleasure to its readers, then the task of compiling it will have been well worthwhile. The other reason for attempting the book grew increasingly important as the work progressed and that is the documenting of a passing phase in the Saudi Arabian people's history. It is the greatest reward to have my book about Bedouin traditional body ornament enjoyed by the Saudi Arabian people themselves.

The commentary does not amount to a scholarly work but it does take into account carefully coordinated information gleaned from the Bedouin, various published sources and the documented information of several authorities on Bedouin culture. Where offered details conflicted, no definite claims are made.

Acknowledgements

I am now in the difficult position which has confronted so many before me: wishing to express appreciation to the people who have helped an author publish a first book for which the material is drawn from many sources.

Few books are the work of one person. The help and encouragement of friends are invaluable. In the case of this book, it would be impossible to mention everyone although my gratitude is no less sincerely felt than to those I do mention.

I wish to express my special gratitude to Dr. Abdullah Masri, then Assistant Deputy Minister for Cultural Affairs, Kingdom of Saudi Arabia, who gave me constructive criticism and guidance, and wrote the Foreword.

Sincere thanks go also to Dr. Fouad Abdul-Salam Al-Farsy, the Minister of Information for the Kingdom of Saudi Arabia, for his encouragement and learned advice and to Dr. Abdulaziz H. al-Sowayyegh then of the University of Riyadh, who checked the manuscript for accuracy in relation to Saudi Bedouin traditions. My thanks also go to Keith Carmichael for his encouragement, for offering good advice and an excellent courier service with reference books; to the charming Mrs. Georgette Kashisho for her translations; and to Ralph J. Roberts of the United States Geological Survey team for his time and information.

As my work progressed, I was surprised to see how much was entailed in the production of a quality publication, and I am sure it could only have been achieved with the friendly cooperation of the skilled graphic artist Anthony Nelthorpe and my printer: Bert van der Lisdonk, who constantly seeks perfection. For proof-reading, the most tedious task of all I give my thanks to Natalie Skariatine, and to my best friend, my husband, Barry, who has encouraged me in my creative endeavours since we first met. I also thank our son, Courtenay, for his understanding. And finally, most sincerely, thank you Richard Hartland.

INTRODUCTION

Archaeologists' discoveries reveal that man has always worn some form of jewellery – a fact which suggests that the desire for self-adornment is profound. Since prehistoric times jewellery has had religious significance and superstitious associations; ancient peoples wore amuletic jewellery to protect themselves against misfortunes and the displeasure of their gods in the belief that their ornaments possessed magical powers. Today, many people wear an amuletic ornament of some kind, attesting further to the depth of jewellery's meaning for man.

Throughout the ages, mankind has accorded jewellery a special importance. He has associated it with all the aspects of life with which he is most concerned: money, power, religion and love.

As an art form, the criterion for jewellery is that it must be both beautiful and precious. Traditionally, the patrons of the jewellery craftsmen have been the wealthy, and the exclusive castes. Today, everyone is able to own some form of jewellery, even if it is only a timepiece: sometimes regarded merely as a functional necessity, a watch is invariably chosen for its styling as well as its usefulness. Yet, even now, fine jewellery remains the most obvious expression of status and wealth, because rare and expensive materials are almost always used in its manufacture, and hand-crafted pieces of the highest quality have been seriously affected by recent escalating costs of production.

Social change and mass-production techniques may have allowed everybody to possess jewellery; but rich or poor, the reasons for wearing jewel adornments remain constant – vanity, superstition, sentiment and romance. These universal motives may safely be attributed to the Bedouin woman. She is proud of jewellery which proclaims her a woman of property, making her secure in the knowledge that she has negotiable savings of her own. The ornaments given to her on the occasionof her wedding are her treasure. Her dreams may be of a romantic nature, too, amidst the mundane practicality of survival in the desert. It is also important to record that custom and tradition play prime roles in the acquisition and wearing of an Arabian Bedouin woman's jewellery.

Heather Colyer Ross

7

FOREWORD

Body ornament is an ancient art in Arabia. Numerous petroglyphs and pictographs have been found on rock faces throughout Saudi Arabia which depict human figures adorned with necklaces and head ornaments, and surrounded by camels, ibexes and palm trees – the natural setting for the desert nomads. Some of the rock art scenes are well over seven thousand years old. Clearly, early and modern Bedouins derive their fashions and use of jewellery from deep roots.

Our understanding of the traditional Bedouin way of life and custom is still shrouded by obscurity and sometimes confounded by fanciful and romantic images. Accurate descriptive ethnography of Bedouin society is woefully scant, in spite of the voluminous accounts of the early travellers and explorers of Arabia.

In their traditional nomadic culture, the Bedouin of Arabia rarely if ever practised artisan work: rather, they engaged the services of artisan classes, such as silversmiths, who had a secondary status within the tribal structure. These specialized service groups were frequently drawn from the semi-sedentary town folk. Once attached to a certain nomadic group, they became affiliated to its tribal organization and catered exclusively to its needs. Parallel to this arrangement, many Bedouin groups sought these services directly from established specialists in sedentary communities. With the weakening of tribal organization in recent history, the latter pattern has gradually become predominant. In either case, the significant point is that Bedouin crafts, especially jewellery, have always been the product of sedentary people and tailored to the specific social and cultural predilections of the nomads.

This illustrated account of Bedouin jewellery treats recent examples, particularly those of Central Arabia. The author provides very useful descriptions and classifications of the various ornamental jewellery common in the markets of the major towns. She also discusses some of the relevant traditions and beliefs associated with its use.

The presentation should be a delight to anyone enamoured of the attractive simplicity and colourfulness of Bedouin jewellery. It could also prove very useful for future work on the wider social and cultural implications of this feature of Bedouin life. It is a fervent hope, echoed by the countless students of Bedouin culture, that a proper appreciation of this important element of Middle Eastern life will yet emerge, despite the increasingly ominous signs of its actual passing.

Dr Abdullah H. Masry
*Assistant Deputy Minister
for Cultural Affairs,
Kingdom of Saudi Arabia 1978*

THE BEDOUIN 1

Their heritage

MESOPOTAMIA, the cradle of civilization, was the site of one of the earliest and greatest civilizations of mankind. Mesopotamia is a Greek coinage for "between rivers", indicating its geographical location between the Tigris and Euphrates rivers which flow into the Arabian Gulf. This civilization of the Fertile Crescent, the territorial horseshoe north of the Arabian Peninsula, flourished from the fifth to the second millenia BC, comprising the successive empires of Sumer, Babylonia, Assyria and Chaldea. It was there that some of the most important cultural and technical advances of the ancient world were made. Today it is southern Iraq.

Recent archaeological discoveries within Saudi Arabia point to a heritage linked with Mesopotamia. The findings suggest that the ancient people of the eastern and northern flanks of Arabia, attracted to this fertile land, may well have contributed to the shaping of Mesopotamia. Until these dramatic revelations, the earliest history of the Arabian people was obscure, Now, Muslim scholars, armed with new archaeological evidence, are confidently seeking to fill in the details of their ancestors.

The first high culture in southern Arabia is evident circa 1400 BC, and appears to have been introduced by colonists from the Fertile Crescent. The Curator of Old World Archaeology at the Smithsonian Institution, Gus van Beek, writes in *The Rise and Fall of Arabia Felix*, that a search for wealth may have been the prime factor which caused Northern Semites to move to southern Arabia. It appears that they migrated mainly for the development of the frankincense and myrrh markets. These Semite immigrants, he continues, were probably adept at metallurgy when they first settled in the region, because by 1200 BC the technology of bronze alloying had been known for one thousand years in the Near East, and iron was becoming widely used in the Fertile Crescent. Throughout the last millenium BC, bronze technology was also highly advanced in southern Arabia.

Their history

The prosperity of early Arabia is well documented. While fabulous wealth was derived from its location within the ancient world as the "gateway to the East", the peninsula thrived in its important role in trade and commerce.

As a land of abundance, South-western Arabia was known to the Romans as Arabia Felix: "contented" or "fortunate" Arabia. It was a contented Arabia, perhaps, because – as archaeologists have found – its cities and towns were unfortified. The reason for their peaceful existence may

Because of the wide demand for frankincense and myrrh and their limited supply, the price was driven up, and in Biblical times their cost ranked with gold.

Trade with southern Arabia also comprised spices, silks, ivory and other valuable commodities destined for Egypt and Mediterranean lands. Since the sources of these goods – India, East Africa and the Indies – were unknown at first-hand to the consumers, Arabia was able to carry out a highly profitable trade. Arabia also supplied the northern countries in the Near East with gold, copper and

possible. The animal's anatomical limitations largely dictated the line that the trade routes took, because the camel is exceptionally top-heavy when loaded and its feet are not suited to rocky ground. Since it is not an effective beast of burden in mountainous regions the best camel routes follow relatively level ground of sand or soil.

The caravan routes can be traced across the plateau and through the valleys to the east of the high mountains of south west Arabia. The camels were formed into long trains which carried the rich cargoes

have been due to comparative isolation. It was "fortunate" in that, as van Beek points out, southern Arabia was the source of the finest frankincense and myrrh. These highly prized resins had many uses in the ancient world. During Roman times it was customary to burn frankincense in the funeral pyre of royal and noble persons whilst myrrh was used primarily in cosmetics, perfumes and as an enbalming agent; both were used also for medicaments, unguents and temple incense.

precious stones. Some of the gold and copper came from Arabia itself where rich mines existed. Western Arabia, for long a source of semi-precious stones, provided gemstones.

Gus van Beek states that the time of the Semites' migration to southern Arabia and the start of the major trade in frankincense and myrrh coincided with the domestication of the camel. This significant development in transportation circa 1400 BC made travel and cargo carrying over vast stretches of arid lands

under heavy guard – a spectacular and familiar part of the early Arabian scene. The caravaneers were drawn from different tribes: nomads who were careful to maintain friendly neutrality in their relations with tribesmen whose territory they crossed.

Frankincense and myrrh were also transported by sea. In the ninth centry BC the fleet of King Solomon [c.970–944], under Pheonician management, is thought to have transported these commodities to the Fertile Crescent. Arab vessels carried them westward to the Arabian Gulf and also up the Red Sea to Egypt throughout the first millennium BC. Many of the caravan routes were to remain in use to the present day but the prosperity of the area was destined to come to an end. The economic decline of Arabia began in the first century BC with an invasion of the covetous Romans, and this trend was accelerated by both the Greeks and Romans who learned the secrets of the monsoon winds and acquired the Arabs' navigational skills,

reduced. The flow of wealth in reciprocal trade to Southern Arabia was sharply reduced and the land became gradually more and more isolated.

Many scholars have attributed some of the blame for this decline of wealth to the collapse of the Marib Dam. A key feature, van Beek writes, of the superior culture in southern Arabia, was its sophisticated irrigation system. The largest and most famous of the irrigation works was the great dam at Marib, located in present day northern Yemen.

thus destroying their trading monopoly.

Some historians calculate the beginning of the economic decline of Arabia Felix to have occurred as late as the fourth century AD. Many factors contributed. One was undoubtedly the economic loss suffered when the frankincense market collapsed.

The Roman Emperor, Constantine, embraced Christianity, in 323 AD and proclaimed it the State religion of the Roman Empire. Thus simpler burials became popular and the demand for frankincense and myrrh was sharply

Marib was the capital of the Kingdom of Saba, biblical Sheba, from early in the first millenium BC. Five separate kingdoms flourished in Southern Arabia during this period but they did not prosper simultaneously. The Marib Dam was built across the Wadi Dhana in the first millennium BC of earth, faced with stone, sections of which can be seen today. It was unique because its great length of 600 metres spanned the floor between two sluices and diverted water from flash floods into a system of canals which irrigated 4,000 acres. It is generally held that its collapse in the sixth century AD was caused by massive silting.

In the seventh century AD, once again the Arabian Peninsula entered history when the Prophet Mohammed, 570–632 AD, introduced Islam, "submission" to the will of God. After persecution in his birthplace, Mecca, Mohammed went to Medina in 622 AD. The Islamic calendar, the Hijiri begins with this event, the "Hijrah". Late in his life, when his teachings were widely accepted throughout Arabia, Mohammed began to extend his work beyond the borders of Arabia. After his death, the successive leaders of Islam, known as Caliphs or *Khalifat* [which means successors] continued to expand the Islamic empire, spreading throughout the Middle East, North Africa and much of southern Asia. The Caliphs transferred their capital from Medina to Damascus and later to Baghdad. The Peninsula was then relegated to the status of a province and relative obscurity, dignified chiefly by possession of the two Holy Cities, Mecca and Medina.

Ruled from Baghdad, the Islamic Empire rejoiced in a Golden Age. Art, science, philosophy, mathematics, literature and all the creative skills of the hand developed and flourished there. The Crusades, which began in 1096 AD and persisted for three hundred years, were responsible to some extent for bringing European civilization and culture into contact with that of the thriving Islamic Empire, but otherwise left it surprisingly unaffected. See Timeline Pages 120/121.

It was the disastrous Mongol invasion of 1258 AD under Hulagu Khan which shattered this great Empire, slaughtering untold thousands, razing magnificent cities to the ground and laying waste enormous areas of fertile land. The Mongols' destructive force was felt again between 1393 AD and 1402 AD under the leadership of the infamous Tamerlane. These events left the Peninsular people in hardship as well as obscurity; and they suffered still further from frequent internal strife.

The downward trend of misfortunes began to change for Arabia, when Abd al-Aziz ibn Saud (1880-1953) the son of an Emir, or Arab Chieftain, who had been forced into exile by a rival family, devoted himself from the age of twenty to restoring the earlier political eminence of his tribe and to uniting the people of the Arabian Peninsula under one banner.

The story of Ibn Saud, as he became known, is full of drama and romance but, most important of all, it is a story of success. In 1902, he led a small band of armed men to surprise and capture Riyadh. Neighbouring Bedouin tribes

were impressed by his valour and success and rallied to his banner. His dream to unite true believers of Islam, despite their tribal affiliations, began to be realized by means of military campaigns, marriage alliances and social reform. 1913 saw the first withdrawal of the Turkish garrisons from the Peninsula, and the First World War ended the Ottoman Empire. In 1924, Ibn Saud entered Mecca for the first time, wearing the humble garb of a pilgrim, and the following year he reopened the country to other pilgrims, guaranteeing them safe passage to the Holy Cities. In 1926, he was proclaimed King of the Hijaz, and in 1927 he became King of the Hijaz and Najd and its dependencies. Finally, in 1932, he proclaimed that his united realm was to be called the Kingdom of Saudi Arabia.

The most far-reaching event in the modern history of Arabia was the discovery of oil in the 1930s. Economic development impelled by the growth of the oil industry has been remarkably rapid and most nomadic Bedouin have now been introduced to Western technology and material culture, having taken the results of trade with the West into their tent dwellings.

Throughout their turbulent history, the Bedouin's great virtue of social courtesy has remained constant: paradoxically the inhospitable deserts produced a people who exemplified perfect hospitality, the trait becoming so characteristic that knowledge of this gracious tradition reached the outside world from a land which remained otherwise virtually unknown until this century.

Today, in their vast oil resources, Saudi Arabians have found a new basis for wealth. The wheel of fortune has now turned full circle so that the Peninsula thrives once again and trade with the outside world is of great importance – bringing the Peninsular people under the gaze of the curious West. The world has come to know that the Kingdom of Saudi Arabia, new as a political unit, is built upon the values of an ancient society and remains strongly committed to these standards and to the tenets of Islam. It is symbolic of the desire to preserve such values that museums are being established throughout the Kingdom to record and display all aspects of historic and ethnic interest.

Their land

The Arabian Peninsula is a unified plateau tipped slightly towards the east, with a line of rugged mountains in the extreme west which run parallel to the Red Sea coast. The gradual drop toward the Arabian Gulf is broken only by the escarpment of the low Tuwaiq mountains which extend along a west-facing crescent north and south of Riyadh. Much of the land surface is sand-covered: forming the three great deserts of the Nafud, the Dahna and the Rub al-Khali. Outside the deserts the surface is gravel or, in limited areas of the west-central region, jumbled beds of ancient lava. The climate is hot and dry although the Asir highlands along the Red Sea receive enough rain to permit some non-irrigated cultivation. Wadis, the beds of seasonal rivers, mark the course of ancient rivers which still lead the rare

rains down to the plains. Scattered oases, drawing water from springs and wells, permitted some settled agriculture in the past. Today, with modern irrigation, agricultural farming exists on a much larger scale.

Way of life

For centuries the arid and largely desert peninsula remained sparsely peopled by nomadic Bedouin. The word "Bedouin" means desert dweller. These hardy and tenacious desert people, formed by a harsh environment, raised animals for food and transport as well as for trade. Their existence depended on the need of pasture and water for these animals. With such limited arable land, a meagre rainfall, and a lack of sufficient permanent water except at widely separated oases, their search for pasture and water was unrelenting. The semi-nomadic people spent the hottest months of the year in the vicinity of the oases or in the uplands, moving out into the plateau in search of grass only in the late winter and spring. The rare and brief rain can transform a section of desert by germinating long dormant seeds into vegetation, some species of which can survive for several years without further rainfall. The great sand deserts are almost waterless and have always been uninhabited save for wandering Bedouin tribes searching for pasture.

Bedouin savings are traditionally invested in additional livestock and silver jewellery. The jewellery is often used in commercial dealings in the desert town *suqs*, which are the bazaars in the central

market places and gathering spots for settled inhabitants and visiting Bedouin alike. Customarily the *suq* was the temporary camping ground for Bedouin trading their livestock for coffee, tea, rice and other needs. In isolated rural areas the *suq* usually gathers only once a week, and the various *suqs* in any region are held on a different day of the week so that they can be attended in succession by the traders. Despite the advent of money, barter in some *suqs* is still common.

As we have seen, it is generally the settled Bedouin, concentrated at the oases and coastal towns, who make the handicrafts. The traditional handicraft industries include weaving, dyeing, embroidering of cloth, mat and basket weaving, pottery making [particularly water jugs], leatherwork, wood carving, and the smithing of gold, silver and other metals for cooking utensils, jewellery and daggers with sheaths studded with semi-precious stones. These products are seldom exported. Export industries include leather tanning, food processing, date packing and soap making, which also supply commodities for local consumption. Maritime industries used to consist of pearl-fishing and gathering of coral which supplied the needs of the Bedouin jewellery craftsmen. All Bedouin industry, and particularly the handicrafts, have not recovered from a general decline in the 1950s, which was caused by the impact of cheap imported manufactured items, and the loss of labour to the oilfields.

In bartering for his needs, time is of little consideration to the Bedouin and

13

the personal exchange between buyer and seller is highly ritualized. Much satisfaction is derived from the bargaining process which provides an opportunity for those concerned to demonstrate their skill in concluding transactions. They can also exchange gossip and opinions at the same time. After a number of proposals and counter-proposals, agreement on a price is reached; the cleverer bargainer gains both social prestige and the gratification of having made a good transaction.

Social structure

For centuries in the desert regions kinship was the primary organizing principle, with the patrilineal extended family composed of related lineages tracing descent from a common ancestor. These extended families formed the basic social and economic units. They constituted relatively independent groups, some large with thousands of members, and others small consisting of only a few lineages. In most tribes the claim of common descent can no longer be substantiated but in a few important ones the genealogies are carefully preserved. Each lineage is headed by a *shaikh* who makes decisions framed by the consensus of the male family heads of the group. The *shaikh* is usually chosen from a particular family in which the right to provide leadership is inherited. A tribal *shaikh* holds *majlis*, to hear the opinions of the senior members of his tribe.

The most cohesive tribes in Arabia are found among the nomadic Bedouin where each unit usually herds the animals owned by its constituent extended families in a certain territory. In the past, they banded together with other tribes only in response to particular political or economic conditions such as in times of war, when large numbers of tribesmen would gather under a particular leader, or in summer, when hundreds of tents from one or more tribes might congregate at a large well or oasis.

The Bedouin's social structure and mode of living changed little over the centuries, imbued with the ancient values and simplicity of life. Then, in 1932, following the unification of the tribes by Ibn Saud, a spirit of wider brotherhood was engendered. Although the tribes had always shared their common heritage and conviction in Islam, this new allegiance gave them a sense of nationhood for the first time. The Bedouin are intensely conscious of their Islamic heritage and have strong loyalty to their King as the *Imam*, Leader of the Faithful and protector of the shrines of Islam.

In recent years, since the development of the oil industry, the Arabian Bedouin's tribal structure has been weakened by the gradual settlement of both nomads and semi-nomads in the villages and the cities. Whether nomadic or settled, however, the Bedouin's characteristic and legendary courtesy, rooted so deeply in the customs and traditions of centuries, remains rigidly upheld.

Family life

Marriages are generally arranged within the kin group by the parents, on behalf of the young people. The prospective Bedouin husband makes a bridal payment to the father of the girl before the marriage is consummated, often paid in kind rather than in cash. Customarily, the payment is mostly used for the purchase of clothing for the bride, articles for her new house, livestock, jewellery, and other investments for her future security.

It is considered desirable that Bedouin girls should marry before their sixteenth birthday and boys usually between the ages of sixteen and eighteen. Physical beauty and a pleasant disposition are sought in a bride but family prestige is also considered. Proper social status and satisfactory material circumstances are regarded as an essential foundation for a successful marriage and the belief is held that affection should grow out of a marriage, not precede it. It is most important also that the bride should be a virgin before marriage and a faithful wife afterwards, for disgrace and dishonour otherwise falls upon her family.

The marriage is regarded as a civil contract and the ceremony is presided over by the tribal *shaikh* or a respected member of the tribe. The marriage celebration frequently occurs in two stages, one at the home of the girl's family and one at the bridegroom's home where the couple usually go to live. Occasionally the newlyweds will live apart from the bridegroom's family, but close by. The occasion is one of mingled sadness and excitement for the girl's relatives. She is leaving them to join another family, but in taking her place as a member of the community she is

bringing honour to her own people. During the ceremony the bride is seated in an elevated place so that her bridal clothes, jewellery and appearance may be observed and applauded by all present. Music, dancing and singing, as well as the serving of sweetmeats or even a full banquet, are part of the celebration at the bride's home; friends and relatives of the bridegroom usually come to escort the bride to her new home, where there is more feasting.

Such marriages are normally entered into with the expectation that they will last for the lifetime of the partners, but it is not insisted upon that they should be preserved under all circumstances. There is no disgrace in divorce. Many adults have two or three marriages in their lifetime. Most are monogamous but some men do have two or more wives at one time, being allowed four wives under Islamic law so long as the husband observes the Koranic injunction that he treats his wives equally.

Relations between husband and wife are characterized by respect and consideration, and if the man takes more than one wife, he is expected to maintain each in separate quarters. Sometimes, however, a second wife is brought into the household of the first wife and generally they get along well together, sharing household tasks and responsibilities.

The husband, nominally, makes the decisions, including marriage arrangements, but generally after discussions with the family. Activities within the home, however, are under the authority of the wife. She has responsibility for their children, daughters-in-law, and to some extent the men themselves in the organization of household routines. For all practical purposes, women's activities are confined to the home; but should women go out in public, they are usually chaperoned by a servant or male member of the family.

Large families are desired as children are regarded as bringing a blessing on the home. A common felicitation is "may you have many children". Special value is placed on sons amongst the Bedouin for they will add to the reputation of the family, whereas daughters will "build someone else's house", Although marriage itself confirms the maturity of the individuals involved, only upon the birth of a son are the parents regarded as "complete" adults. Symbolic acknowledgement of the importance of this event is signified by a change in the names by which the parents are known. Among friends and relatives, parents are thereafter addressed as the father or the mother of so-and-so, using the first name of the son.

From the time that they are able, Bedouin children begin to help with the work of the household and the girls are expected to care for their younger brothers and sisters. After the age of eight or thereabouts, boys are more in the company of their fathers, whilst girls keep company with other females within the home. Young people of both sexes are expected to look after their elders.

The extended family system has traditionally handled the problems of the needy, the aged and ill, the handicapped and divorced, and the widowed and orphaned: all these unfortunates are cared for by more fortunate members of the family. An individual in need of economic aid or protection is expected to turn to his kinsmen. The emergence of Islam in the seventh century, whilst not altering fundamentally the traditional pattern, superimposed a concept of broader responsibility. Muslims accept inequalities of talent and wealth as ordained by God and they insist on the moral obligations of the richer and more fortunate members of the community to assist and support the poor.

In the typical nomadic household, the day begins with the first prayer just before dawn. After a light breakfast the day's activities commence: household work and meal preparation for the girls and women, and work outside for the boys and men. Care of their camels is of vital importance and they are often very fond of their particular favourites. Women's tasks include the spinning of domestic goat hair or camel hair, the yarn often being sold for weaving by the settled Bedouin, although some rugs and camel bags are made by nomadic Bedouin, as is the rough woven cloth of the tents. Nomadic tribesmen sometimes do leatherwork for their own needs, but as a general rule crafts are performed by the artisan class. A large tribe, as we have seen, often employs its own craftsmen, drawn from the settled areas and these artisans become part of the tribal structure, catering to that tribe's needs solely.

The Bedouin diet consists mainly of milk and milk products from goats, sheep and camels, together with dates, rice, or, less frequently, wheat. Milk is drunk fresh or curdled into yoghourt or cheese. Coffee and tea are the favourite beverages. Meat is eaten only on special occasions, when an animal is slaughtered or when wild game is available. Locusts and the *dabb*, a heavy fleshy lizard, are also consumed. Nomads eat fresh fruit and vegetables only when they visit the villages of settled cultivators. Despite this meagre diet, the Bedouin generally have considerable physical endurance.

The largest meal of the day is served in the evening, as Bedouin men usually do not return home at midday. This meal is a family affair unless there are guests present who are not close relatives. In such a case the men are served apart from the women and children. Before the meal, there is a long social time. Food is served quite late and friends depart shortly afterwards. The women who have leisure time spend it visiting their friends, but irrespective of how wives spend the late afternoon, they are expected to be home to greet their husbands.

As elsewhere in the Arab world, poetry, formal prose and oratory have long been esteemed the highest of the arts, and they have a special attraction to the Bedouin whose life is essentially spartan. The skilful use of language is valued for itself. A poet is regarded as the possessor of remarkable powers, the repository of tribal history and guide and spokesman for his tribe. In days of old a poet, often a warrior himself, strove to express in his

work the ideals of manliness: gallantry, bravery, loyalty, independence of spirit and generosity. Oral folk literature comprises proverbs, stories, and the narratives of professional story-tellers, whose recitations are particularly in demand during the Muslim month of fasting, *Ramadan*. They provide and perpetuate a wealth of pious, earthy or epic oral literature which has been passed on for countless generations. Much of the poetry contains genealogies and tribal histories.

Popular also is vocal and instrumental music which is part of the poetic tradition. Musical expression on an informal folk level comprises repetitive bars and intricate beats sometimes played with a coffee grinding mortar and pestle. Other instruments are the lute, the zither, the drum, tambourine and the one-stringed fiddle. The famous Arab stringed instrument, the *ud*, is also often part of the group at a concert within a semi-settled area. The ability to improvise a melody constitutes one of the standards by which a performer is judged.

Dancing, although associated with these folk arts, is not generally a group activity, with few exceptions such as the Bedouin sword dance which is performed only on special occasions. However, women do frequently dance amongst themselves. The exceptional circumstances which provide an opportunity for group dancing within the tribe occur on such festive occasions as weddings, circumcisions and religious holidays.

Jewellery as dowry

Dowry, known as *mahr* in Arabic, is a strong tradition amongst the Bedouin, although the form dowry takes varies greatly and is often paid in kind rather than in cash. The *mahr* is generally divided into two sums: the *muqaddam*, or first part, is paid at the time of engagement, and the *muakhkhar*, or second part, is a sum promised to the wife in case of divorce. In case of the death of a husband, the sum is paid from his estate or by his family.

Traditional Bedouin marriages are arranged by the parents on behalf of the young people, the prospective husband making his bridal payment to the father

Bedecked for a special occasion, Bedouin women and girls display their personal wealth of silver jewellery. Worn in the customary profusion, the weight of the ornnments preclude domestic activity. The heaviest single bracelet and anklet weighs approximately two hundred grammes.

of the girl before the marriage is consummated, for it is customary for the bride's father to use some of this payment for the purchase of clothing for the bride, articles for her prospective home, livestock, and jewellery as an investment for her future security.

It is conceivable that a Bedouin would rarely accumulate wealth, with his way of life, and it is equally unlikely that he would spend frivolously should he manage to save any portion. The fact that he buys his daughter silver jewellery as part of her dowry puts the importance of these ornaments in clear perspective.

The engagement contract, the *milak*, drawn up by the fathers of the bride and groom before the Muslim religious leader, the *Imam* and two witnesses, is considered more important than the wedding ceremony. At this time, the bridegroom offers the dowry as his pledge of good faith; the bride's father spends a percentage of this offering on his daughter's silver jewellery which, under Muslim law, becomes the woman's personal wealth; and the Bedouin bride accepts this tribute as her right according to custom and tradition. Her jewellery is worn with pride for it proclaims her new status as a married woman of property, and as it is entirely her own, she may sell it in times of need if she so desires. There must be an element of security engendered by this wise custom. Less practical but no less important to state is that a Bedouin woman, like any other, prizes her jewellery for its decorative role.

Despite the fact that the majority of a Bedouin woman's jewellery, including

rings, is a wedding gift, the giving of a "betrothal" ring is unknown amongst the Bedouin. It is recorded, however, that as far back as the Prophet's time, finger-rings were associated with dowry, and for *mahr*, there exists an Islamic injunction for adherents of the Faith to offer rings to their brides as a minimum presentation. The Bedouin women from central Arabia say that they receive bracelets as marriage tokens today.

The father of the bride may have gone to a settled artisan in a town close by to purchase the quantity of hand-made jewellery required as an acceptable percentage of the *mahr*, or he may have bought it from an itinerant trader or silversmith. It may have been purchased within his extended family. Some of the larger tribes actually employ their own silversmiths to supply their needs. Wherever the source, it is possible that the quality and quantity of the items purchased for his daughter's dowry would be similar to that bought by a neighbour, but the price invested might be more or might be less, depending on the silver content: for it is a common practice for the silversmiths to produce varying qualities to suit all pockets.

The wedding party is generally held in the evening and there is much gaiety although the men and women celebrate separately. It is usual during the marriage celebrations for the bride to be seated in an elevated position where relatives and friends who visit briefly may see and appreciate her appearance and new silver jewellery.

TYPES OF JEWELLERY 2

TRADITIONAL BEDOUIN jewellery from Central Arabia is generally fashioned from silver and often predominently displays turquoise for embellishment, It is interesting to see that races as widely separated as the Saudi Arabians and the Mexicans should choose exactly the same combination of materials for their body ornament. Mexican jewellery is generally more finely fashioned with higher grades of silver and turquoise, but Arabian Bedouin jewellery has singular charms, such as its boldness of design, its substantial size and its distinctively hand-crafted appearance resembling ornaments of the ancients. This combination of characteristics is most appealing, especially to the Westerner whose revived appreciation for hand-crafted items is so evident today. The trend has been much analysed and discussed and seems to be an overt expression of dissatisfaction with highly evolved mass-produced objects which symbolize a decadence in modern civilization, as well as a growing desire to return to a life closer to nature.

Always eye-catching and often exhibiting praiseworthy skill, Arabian Bedouin jewellery's characteristic features include chains; bells; coins; strands of irregular-sized, multi-coloured and silver beads; colourful stones set in simple settings with fluted or beaded surrounds affixed in high-relief; snug-fitting bracelets with hinged openings and pinned fastenings; necklaces affixed with plaited hemp ties; and intricate meshed ornaments, often sewn to cloth backings — perhaps to protect the wearer from the metal, hot from the sun, as much as to preserve the ornament.

The other gems and materials include garnet, carnelian, amber, coral, pearl, agate, glass, faience, plastic, gold and brass.

Bedouin women are rarely seen without their bracelets and a ring or two but the cumbersome inter-linking kaff, *often ajangle with silver bells, and the many other heavy ornaments, are worn only on special occasions.* Kaff, *meaning glove, comprises a ring for one or more fingers, a decorative back-of-hand section, and a bracelet, all held together with chains. There are several styles of* kaff *and some are made of gold.*

21

TRADITIONAL DESIGNS

This fine *iqd*, represents a rare find for it is in its original condition and of fairly high silver content with better workmanship than most other examples now available of this style. The plaited hemp tie, too, is intact although well-worn.

The Bedouin favour traditional styles of jewellery whatever the silver content and workmanship, so this and other items appear in many qualities.

The three cylindrical pendants are charm cases which are called *hirz*. As jewellery components, charm cases have a long history. Similar pendant charm cases were common in Persia in the second and third centuries AD and then had both religious and superstitious significance. They enjoyed a period of popularity again in Persia in the late twelfth and thirteenth centuries.

Hirz are manufactured in a variety of designs and always used as pendants to a necklace in Arabia. Some of the finest examples are crafted in the south of the Peninsula. Unembellished by amuletic red or blue stones and without incised inscription, as shown here, *hirz* are of purely religious import when Koranic verses are sealed inside. Sometimes, however, the receptacle is quite empty.

The natural plaited hemp ties, made of the strands issuing from the triangular silver terminal beads, make this heavy necklace comfortable to wear. The style of necklace is known as *lazem* in Yemen, a name usually given in Saudi Arabia to the ornament worn beard-fashion on the chin line before the neck. See page 99. The multiple strands vary in number but the decoration is invariably 'applied'.

At a time when the number of old silversmiths is decreasing rapidly – and their skills are declining – it is heartening to see valiant attempts to reproduce traditional designs. Favourites, newly-made, seem to be purchased mainly still by the Bedouin, while foreigners search for good examples of old pieces. The design range for old jewellery is broader, of course, which adds to a collector's pleasure.

عقد *iqd*

حرز *hirz*

VALUES

قِيَم

'*llaqahs* are used by Bedouin women to hold their headdresses in place. For decoration and function they are often worn three at a time, one on the back of the head and one at each side, sometimes affixed to a circlet.

Certain head ornaments in Arabia, can be fashioned in fine gold, sometimes imitated in brass. Other traditional pieces are made only in silver, ranging from fine to a poor alloy.

Each '*ilaqah* shown here is strongly made but crudely finished; the four pendant styles, from left to right, show filigree, the embossing technique, hammering, and the use of beads and coins as weights.

Coins, balls, bells and charms are invariably suspended by chains, and these can be unusual. The 'scarab' shape occasionally appears. The scarab is the dung beetle revered by the ancient Egyptians as the symbol of resurrection and immortality, often carved in stone to be worn as jewellery. Later it was also a sacred symbol incorporated into the ornaments of the Etruscans, the race of uncertain origin who came to Italy in the ninth century BC, establishing themselves in what is now Tuscany. The Phoenicians also used the same sacred shapes as the Egyptians, but merely for decoration. The Etruscan reverence for the scarab beetle shape may be a clue to their origin.

Stones, when incorporated into '*ilaqah* design, are traditionally red and blue. The blue stones are sometimes ceramic, *khazaf*, and not turquoise. The red stones can be glass, rather than carnelian or garnet. The silver content is low in the ornaments depicted here, and these pieces would seem to have been produced as inexpensively as possible.

A proportion of cheaper jewellery is generally manufactured to suit the poorer Bedouin's pocket, but the item is no less important to the recipient in its efficacy or its decorativeness. '*llaqahs* come in many designs, and lengths of chains are almost always incorporated, the ornament worn attached to the head-bands by means of a hook. The triangular '*ilaqah* visible here, is an example of the rare design exceptions in Arabian Bedouin jewellery, where the design crosses the shape. It is not known why the beaded wire is used thus rather than to outline and confirm the shape, according to custom.

KORANIC AMULETS

عيمه ديبيه

Occasionally, pieces of Bedouin silver jewellery arrive in Saudi Arabia from outside the Peninsula, testifying to the mobility of these ornaments as the personal wealth of a Bedouin wife. This attractive necklace is one such example and is believed to have been made by an Indian craftsman, due to the more delicate appearance, a characteristic of certain similar Indian jewellery.

The central red stone is a religious amulet, known as a *maskah* or *samakah*, as it is inscribed with the name of Allah, making it, therefore, a Koranic amulet. Many inscriptions read: "Ma sha la" which means "according to God's will". The writing may have been moulded into the red glass or plastic but it is, on silver, gouged out with a tool called a graver, using the decorative technique known as engraving, or *hafr*.

Other Koranic amulets become so by virtue of religious verses which are sealed inside charm cases of varying shape and size. The charm cases are known as *hirz*. However, since they are sealed, it is never certain that they are amuletic.

The flower vase-shape has been made from sheet silver and the embellishment incorporates various elements involving applied filigree and granulation plus the application of beaded wire to accent shape, and applied discs to confirm it.

There are red ceramic beads set in high collets following the design, and red glass, also mounted in high collets on the attractive chain. Additionally, four fixed rings serve to anchor chained pendant balls which cascade over the face of the ornament. Some appear to be missing.

مسكه أو سمكه *maskah or samakah*

حرز *hirz*

ماشاء الله *ma sha la*

حفر *hafr*

CHILDREN'S JEWELLERY

حُلّى الاولاد

Bells, known as *zarir*, as components of Bedouin jewellery, whether attached to bracelets, anklets, belts or rings, are supposed to have originated in Najran, in the south-west of Saudi Arabia, close to the northern Yemen border. Similar bells were used in an identical fashion by the ancient Greeks in the seventh century BC and are worn today by the Turkomans of Afghanistan who believe them to have protective powers and that the tinkling sound will frighten away harmful spirits.

Children's anklets such as the one pictured here are fashioned cleverly and are delightful ornaments; nothing like them appears in Western jewellery. Often, they are hollow, with hinged and pinned fastenings. Similar anklets [*khalakhil*] occur in Oman where they are given to children for protection. Worn merely for decoration or for talismanic function, these anklets are, without a doubt, soothing and interesting play-things.

Talismanic function was once an important aspect of Man's jewellery. Even today, in Syria and Jordan, small charms, *hijab*, are placed on children by their mothers who believe that they will thus be protected from dangers and illnesses. Historically, too, pebbles trapped within the body or terminals of hollow bracelets, armlets and anklets were believed to repel malevolent spirits by their rattling sound. And once again jewellery of ancient purpose can serve a modern child as amusing ornaments. Saudi Arabian Bedouin children, who wear traditional jewellery with design elements similar to ancient ornaments of symbolic meaning, attach no importance to them other than as pleasing possessions.

Although a young nomadic woman may not receive any appreciable quantity of jewellery before marriage, little girls are rarely without ornaments such as necklaces and bracelets.

زرير	*zarir*
خلاخيل	*khalakhil*
حجاب	*hijab*

MULTIPLE PENDANTS

كردله *kirdala*

بدوي *Badawi*

مصري *Masri*

عجمي *Ajami*

The Bedouin choker necklace or pectoral, *kirdala*, depicted here, was purchased in north-east Arabia. It displays several of the characteristics of Bedouin jewellery: multiple pendants, figure-eight links with suspended balls, set red and blue stones, and applied silver-working techniques: filigree and beaded wire have been applied to the choker band which is secured with a simple hook clasp of large proportions. The lozenge-shaped pendant beads and balls have been made in two parts and raised to roundness by the embossing technique prior to being soldered together and decorated with beaded wire. The diamond-shaped plaques affixed to the figure-eight links are decorated with granulation. The tiny disc charms pendant from the neckband are edged with beaded wire.

Multiple pendants are a common design element of Bedouin [*Badawi*] jewellery illustrating an appreciation for ancient style and elegance so often apparent in Bedouin jewellery, This type of necklace was popular with the Egyptian [*Masri*] and Persian [*Ajami*] jewellers in the past.

It is relevant to note that Egyptian influence on modern Western jewellery has become apparent since the opening of Tutankhamun's tomb in 1922, and the subsequent world-wide exhibitions of the jewellery that was discovered. By contrast, Persia's artistic vitality has continued steadily down through the ages since the conquest of the Persian Empire by Alexander the Great, circa 330 BC, expressing itself again and again in jewellery crafted during the rise and fall of subsequent civilizations as one culture enriched another.

Pendants are usually geometrically-shaped but some display pendant motifs which were perhaps inspired by the moon: the crescent shape and a circle, the symbol of the full phase of the moon. The moon [*badr*] is often romanticized by the great poets of Islam – the night of the full moon is for lovers.

Modern jewellers may draw upon any or several cultures when seeking inspiration for ornament design, but it is rare today to see hand-made jewellery, such as that worn by the Arabian Bedouin, of styles which astonishingly span thousands of years.

BRACELETS, ANKLETS & BELTS

أحزمة وخلاخِل وأساوِر

أساور	*asawir*
خلاخيل	*khalakhil*
أحزمة	*ahzimah*
شرقي	*Sharqi*

Bracelets, known as *asawir*, and anklets, *khalakhil*, are often worn in matched sets. The anklets are somewhat larger in diameter than the bracelets, and they are sometimes flexible, with hinged and pinned fastenings. Bracelets, as hoops or horse-shoe shapes, are invariably rigid; sometimes the former having hinged and pinned closures.

It is recorded that the daughter of the Prophet Mohammed, Fatima, received two silver anklets in her dowry.

Belts, *Ahzimah*, differ in style regionally. A most appealing silver belt is the *Raad*, which means thunder, due to the very loud noise it makes when the wearer dances and sets the large bells jangling.

The belt, *hizam*, depicted here weighs more than two kilos, and together with a tribal lady's bracelets, anklets, necklaces and rings, worn for festive occasions, the total weight is considerable. Fringed with silver balls, charms and bells, the wearing of this boldly-designed jewellery adds to the enjoyment of the swaying Bedouin dance. It is also a particularly Oriental, [*Sharqi*] characteristic to include tiny objects in hollow jewellery to rattle rhythmically with a dancer's movements.

Red glass beads are set in high silver collets and also hang from some of the interesting pendants. The hooked closure plaque clasps and belt plaque segments are cast. Most belts in Arabia are flexible and made of silver in all qualities. Some are gilded. One belt worn in the west and south-west comprises a broad leather and cloth base, totally oversewn with silver beads and buttons. It is secured by leather thong loops over silver coin buttons.

EARRINGS, NOSE-RINGS & TOE-RINGS

خِرصان وخزامات

To further adorn themselves, Bedouin women often have one nostril pierced but this is not quite so commonplace as the custom of piercing the ear lobes. The traders of the Bedouin Women's *Suq* in Riyadh today favour tiny gold flower-shaped studs for nose ornamentation. Usually set with turquoise, pearls and red stones, these studs originated in the Indian subcontinent and seem to be preferred at the moment to the traditional cumbersome styles. The small nose ornaments are called *shaf* or *khizama* and the large nose jewels are known as *fraida*.

In the remote Bedouin regions of Saudi Arabia the more traditional nose ornament is the large silver hoop or half-moon worn on one side of the nose. Far to the south-east of the Peninsula, Omani women seem to favour such hoops too, whilst to the west similar half-moon shapes adorn the women of Libya and other countries in North Africa. Both styles were common in Byzantine times and passed into the Islamic world with the spread of the Ottoman Empire.

Identically designed ornaments are used for the ears, but earrings are called *halaq* or *khurs* [plural, *khirsan*]. In Oman, women's ears are sometimes pierced in three places, from near the top of the ear down to the lobe, to display three sets of similar hooped earrings at one time. [Such is currently a fashion in the West among both males and females.]

It is also a Bedouin custom to hook large pendants into the headcloth at the point of the ear-lobes. These are known as *'ilaqah*.

Some are joined to a more comprehensive head ornament, which has

the purpose of holding the headgear in place – see pages 24/25.

Earrings and nose-rings of the styles above and right, are quite rare today; they lost popularity quite some time ago.

Above: This old style of nose-ring or earring varies in that it can be created without pendant bells, but invariably displaying the wired form of decoration known as filigree [*qsir shift* or *mushabbak*] generally employed in the applied form, but occasionally *à jour*. The cylinder body which exhibits applied decoration is 6 centimetres in length. It was created by the technique of embossing.

Opposite: This pair of Central Arabian, Najdi, semi-circular earrings are made from two sheets of thin gold. The front sheets are decorated and the backs are

plain. Some examples in gold or silver exhibit the mark of the maker, but this is rare. When there are set stones, they are blue, and in this case, turquoise and fringed pearls, plus the techniques of filigree and granulation make up the embellishment. The half-circle hoop, once linked to a missing loop-catch.

Toe-rings exist in Arabia, too, usually as larger sizes of some finger-ring styles.

سوق	*suq*
شاف أو خزامه	*shaf or khizama*
فريده	*fraida*
حلق أو خرص	*halaq or khurs (pl. khirsan)*
مشبّك	*qsir shift or mushabbak*

FINGER-RINGS: TURQUOISE

خواتم – فيروز

The hoop of a finger-ring, *khatim*, is called the shank; the decorated upper part, the bezel; and the encompassing band, usually holding a stone, often filed or cut away to make claws, is the collet; and the pieces which are sometimes attached to both shank and bezel, are called shoulders.

Ring craftsmanship often brings all the jewellery-making techniques into play. The shank is sometimes cast but usually wrought. The bezel is invariably decorated and sometimes incorporates a stone, either held by claws or glued inside the encompassing band, which is cut from hammered and annealed metal. The shank and shoulders generally exhibit heavily encrusted relief achieved by several of the decorative techniques.

Bedouin finger-ring styles are many and varied; their large stones, high bezels, richly decorated shanks and shoulders, often incorporating pendanted bells, culminate in bold and colourful pieces of jewellery.

This picture displays the most common designs for Bedouin turquoise rings. All are large, handsome, and crudely fashioned with most collets accentuated by coarse granulation.

Defining the use of Bedouin *khawatim* [finger-rings], is difficult – a problem recognized by eminent authors in the classification of finger-rings of the past. Documentation is lacking, and a ring often serves more than one purpose. In olden times, even in prehistoric times, the main purpose of finger-rings is considered to have been decorative, but they often also had amuletic value. Moreover, they were sometimes worn by tradition on certain fingers for a specific function or symbolic purpose. Even today, in the West, there is a specific finger for the wearing of the wedding ring, although there is no certainty as to where this practice originated and why.

H.R.P. Dickson, a noted Arabist, in his book *The Arab of the Desert*, states that in some Middle Eastern countries, up to four rings are worn on one hand at one time. In Arabia itself, as many as can be managed are worn for festive occasions.

According to Dickson, the names and number and placement of rings vary greatly throughout the Middle East. He gives the following names and placement for Bedouin finger rings in Kuwait: "*Khamzar*, a ring for the little finger; *wasat*, a ring for the third finger, made of silver and gold, set with a large square or oval turquoise stone; thin rings, plain silver or gold, in threes for the second finger, known as *al marami*; and one silver ring on fore-finger with a large square turquoise, named *al shahid*, worn only by the well-to-do Bedouin ladies."

Al shahid is actually the term for the fore-finger in Arabic, so called because a Muslim points this finger when uttering the *shahadah*, the Islamic doctrinal formula. It is possible then that this name came to be applied to other types of rings when worn on the fore-fingers.

The Bedouin women of Central Arabia call these rings *fawariz*, which is obviously derived from the Arabic name for turquoise, *fairuz*.

All the rings shown opposite, some combining gold bezel with silver shank, are worn on the middle fingers in the Central province of Saudi Arabia. The turquoise is almost always fashioned in flat form but occasionally the slightly domed "tallow-topped cobochon" turquoise is found, sometimes set in brass with a silver shank. Old gold rings, often set with a central gold pin, are now extremely rare. Old "flower"-design silver rings set with turquoise petals and red stone pistils, are equally scarce.

خاتم	*khatim*
خنصر	*khamzar*
وسط	*wasat*
المرامي	*al marami*
الشاهد	*al shahid*
شهادة	*shahadah*
فوارز	*fawariz*
فيروز	*fairuz*

FINGER-RINGS: RED STONES

خواتم ـ أحجار حمراء

كف *kaff*

عقيق أحمر *aqiq ahmar*

زجاج *zujaj*

فتحة *fatkhah*

The history of finger-rings is full of fascinating stories. For instance, up until the early seventeenth century, the Pope annually blessed a number of rings to be worn against cramp. Magical properties have long been attributed to jewels and precious stones, partly because, by the lore of contagious magic, anything worn close to the body was assumed to affect its wearer's health. Today, in the Western World many doctors recommend patients to wear copper bracelets, sometimes with inset magnets, for relief from rheumatism. It is quite likely that contact with minerals aids the human body. Undoubtedly, the taking of certain minerals orally in the form of medicine has proven beneficial.

In the Hellenistic period, about the middle of the third century BC, massive finger-rings which included stones wider than the finger were fashionable, and present-day Bedouin women display a similar fondness for this imposing style of ring.

In Roman times a ring was worn on each finger, which is a usual practice of Bedouin women. One attractive piece of Bedouin jewellery consists of five rings, one for each finger and the thumb, all connected by links to a decorative patch on the back of the hand, and secured to a bracelet. This ornament is known as a *kaff* [literally, "glove"]. Sometimes the ancient Romans wore several slender rings, each set with a different stone which they united into one; but generally a single intaglio formed the bezel with tapered shoulders, often ornately carved with an inscription on the shank. A characteristic of Bedouin finger-rings is the use of the filigree on both shank and shoulder, giving them an ornateness similar to that of Roman rings.

Carnelian, often known as cornelian, *aqiq ahmar*, is a quartz of orange to brownish-red colour, and a typical feature of Bedouin rings. The old belled ring at the *top right* demonstrates its use. Those at *left* and *right* are set with garnets, also known in Arabic as *aqiq ahmar*. The low grade silver rings [*front*] are crudely fashioned and roughly set with a glass, *zujaj*, but remain attractive finger-rings.

A red stone ring is often called *fatkhah* [plural *fatakh*].

RETHREADED NECKLACES

قلائد مضمونة

The placing at intervals of large and often silver beads and pendant ornaments is a characteristic of Bedouin necklaces, or *iqd*. Graduated strands are unknown; and strands of beads of uniform size, except in the case of amber, are also not traditional. When such strands appear, it can safely be assumed that they have been rethreaded because the oldest, intact examples of *qiladah*, and *iqd*, always feature beads of varying sizes and colours and a pair of mace-shaped terminal beads.

It is common practice today, for the women jewellery traders to rethread necklaces with a sale in mind rather than traditional design reconstruction. Occasionally, these commercially-minded dealers can be seen at work with a tray of loose beads, threading diligently, using one pendant only for each necklace when tradition dictates multiples.

And, in their trays, there are many pairs of mace-shaped beads. There are several sizes and designs for this obligatory bead; yet, on the completed necklaces, it is common to see a mis-matched pair or none at all.

The largest beads and terminal beads in an Arabian Bedouin necklace are generally of fine *fiddah* [silver], fashioned from sheet metal and often elaborately decorated. The largest beads are created by the method of embossing, requiring two domed halves to be soldered together. Terminal beads and most small beads are made from pieces of silver folded over to meet rather than solid drilled metal.

Because of the weight of the beads and pendants, necklaces probably break quite often, and most would therefore have been reconstructed many times.

Despite the crude execution of this amulet pendant, the ornament as a whole is elegant. A necklace of this type, a pendant in the true sense, is called *qiladah*. Its simplicity is interesting because charm cases such as this usually appear with other pendants on a single necklace. And, such a strand does not normally appear with this pendant – the large silver beads at regular intervals are traditionally interspersed with smaller, coloured beads. However, the mace-shaped beads, to be expected in terminal position, do match the beads, and the threading seems original. It is assumed that a modern, innovative silversmith designed this attractive necklace. The charm case features applied decoration.

On the thread visible between the five embellished suspension loops at the top of the charm case, and on the thread anchoring the pendant balls at the base of the chains, red beads are commonly threaded, a characteristic throughout Bedouin jewellery. Often they are coral.

عقد   *iqd*
قلاده   *qiladah*
فضّة   *fiddah*

BEZEL DESIGN

تصميم قاعدة فصّ الخاتم

مهر *mahr*

Arabian Bedouin women do not traditionally receive rings as a symbol of betrothal, although the majority of a Bedouin women's jewellery comes to her effectively as a wedding gift. However, as far back as the Prophet Mohammed's time, finger-rings were associated with weddings and *mahr* [dowry] for there exists an Islamic instruction for Muslims to offer rings to their brides as a minimum presentation.

Betrothal rings first appeared in ancient Roman times and have continued down through the ages as a symbol of marriage, although the forms of marriage rings have changed over the centuries. The plain bands of today are a relatively new innovation and the custom of exchanging them very recent indeed. The exchange of rings between husband and wife, or at least the supplying of a wedding band to the bride, is now customary in Saudi Arabia.

Amongst the Bedouin finger-ring range, the bezel, or decorated upper portion, is usually large and often set high. The collet is necessarily practical and hardy – and for added security, the stone is laid on a bed of sticky pitch. This serves also to cushion an uneven gem base. Furthermore, some stones are also secured by a central pin. It is characteristic for the pin, collet and shoulders to be ornate.

The set of five high-bezel, coral-coloured, and silver-pinned, ceramic bead and silver rings are from Najran, south-west Saudi Arabia. In times past, women of the region wore such rings on fingers and toes, as well as pendants from their necklaces and clothing. In matched sets of five, these rings can be seen threaded on a local turban, made up of a thick rope of stranded black wool. Some fine examples of this style of ring are set with coral. The stones can be reddish-brown carnelian, red ceramic or pink opaque glass. The bezels and shanks, from fine silver to a poor silver-metal alloy, are invariably richly worked with filigree and granulation.

3 HISTORICAL INFLUENCES

FROM THE written records of the Mesopotamian and Assyrian dynasties, it is known that the Arabian Bedouin used both gold and silver since ancient times; these records mention tributes and gifts brought by Bedouin chiefs from North Arabia. Further evidence attesting to the long history of silver and gold body ornament in Arabia was found in a pre-Islamic tomb at Jawan in the Eastern Province. Accurate dating of the burial was difficult as water had entered the area. However, it is set at circa 100 AD.

The beads of the necklace shown (*right*), were retrieved unstrung from about the neck of the body's remains. Mr. F.S. Vidal, the archaeologist responsible for the excavation, writes a description: "The position of the beads found indicated that the girl had been wearing a necklace made of a variety of stones: garnet, carnelian, amethyst, onyx, and pearls, and a few small gold beads in a variety of shapes, bulbar, annular, cylindrical, mace-shaped, and two imitating cowrie shells."

Two other items of beautiful jewellery were found in the grave but as yet there are no comparable pieces of ancient jewellery from the Arabian Peninsula. Apart from the elaborate, finely-crafted gold jewellery, there was a purplish colouration on the clay in several parts of the tomb that proved to be silver chloride. From this it has been concluded that the excavated body had worn silver ornaments on the head and breast of which nothing but stained clay has remained. Small pieces of purplish coloured metal also found there may have been fragments of silver finger-rings.

Experts believe that although as much silver jewellery as gold may have been worn in the ancient world, all but a few pieces have perished because silver tarnishes when exposed to sulphur compounds in the air – an oxidization process which ultimately destroys the metal. Gold, by contrast, is remarkably stable and impervious to the ordinary processes of corrosion and decay, allowing a study of ancient gold body ornament.

The majority of Bedouin ornaments in circulation today are silver, although a few items such as buttons, beads, rings and forehead pieces are made of gold. It is rare that any of this gold and silver jewellery is more than fifty years old, as it is usually melted down after the death of its owner in accordance with tradition, to be sold as silver or reworked into new pieces. One may presume that the reason for old jewellery being melted down is that, as the personal property of a Bedouin wife, given to her as dowry, it would be unacceptable to a bride. Moreover, during a married life-time it is likely that the jewellery would show signs of wear and possibly damage.

Craftsmen still produce Bedouin jewellery throughout Arabia, but a number of the artisans are retiring and the younger generation are turning to more profitable occupations. These facts, combined with the Saudi Arabian Bedouin's new preference for mass-produced gold, provide reasons for the disappearance of traditional Bedouin ornaments.

In the past, particularly before the advent of Islam, Bedouin men, too, often wore heavy jewellery. Islamic prophetic tradition enjoined male Muslims, however, not to wear ornaments made of gold or highly precious stones. Only silver was permitted. Some have claimed that Muslim women are permitted to wear only silver ornamentation, but this view has been refuted by learned scholars of Islam. Yet, the fact remains that the majority of traditional Bedouin women's jewellery is fashioned of silver. Perhaps, like Scandinavians today, the beauty of silver has appealed more than gold to the eye of the Bedouin of Arabia in the past.

The Bedouin have obviously now been influenced by the essentially urban predilection for gold. Since jewellery for the nomadic people has always been, as a portable commodity, an ideal form of savings account, the obvious economics of gold versus silver must also have become apparent to the Bedouin.

Jewellery-making techniques and styles of body ornament have been, of course, subject to many influences through the ages. From time to time innovations are introduced from beyond the world of the craftsman through commerce or through the clash or amalgamation of civilizations. Thus all art forms can be enriched, and jewellery is no exception. It would seem that the comparative isolation in which the Arabians lived following their economic eclipse of almost two thousand years duration is responsible for the Peninsula artisans retaining their ancient jewellery-making techniques and styles; and the purity of expression with which the jewellery is reproduced, albeit with a boldness of interpretation, must also be

44

attributed to this isolation. There are signs too, that jewellers of times past actively sought inspiration for ornament design.

Arabian Bedouin jewellery is tremendously exciting for a unique reason: its technique and styles bear striking resemblance to jewellery of civilizations long dead. For example, the traditional mace-shaped terminal bead of so many of today's Bedouin necklaces is identical to that found [in 1952] in the tomb at Jawan, eastern Saudi Arabia, although the Jawan terminal beads are gold and today's terminal beads are silver.

The British Museum records that "the Islamic world inherited the jewellery techniques and styles of Graeco-Roman Syria and Egypt and of Sassanian Persia, with the earliest surviving examples from Fatimid Egypt and Seljuk Persia" and the decorative styles "developed under the patronage of the Seljuk Turks", wherein "fine silver-gilt and nielloed ornaments were worn". "Islamic" here refers to Syrian and Jordanian jewellery, for the Arabian craft does not include niello and gilding silver is not common. It is clear, therefore, that another facet of Islamic body ornament demands consideration, namely Arabian Bedouin.

This necklace was found in the tomb of a young girl buried in a Seleucid tomb complex, ten kilometres south-west of Ras Tanura in the Eastern Province of Saudi Arabia, in pre-Islamic times.

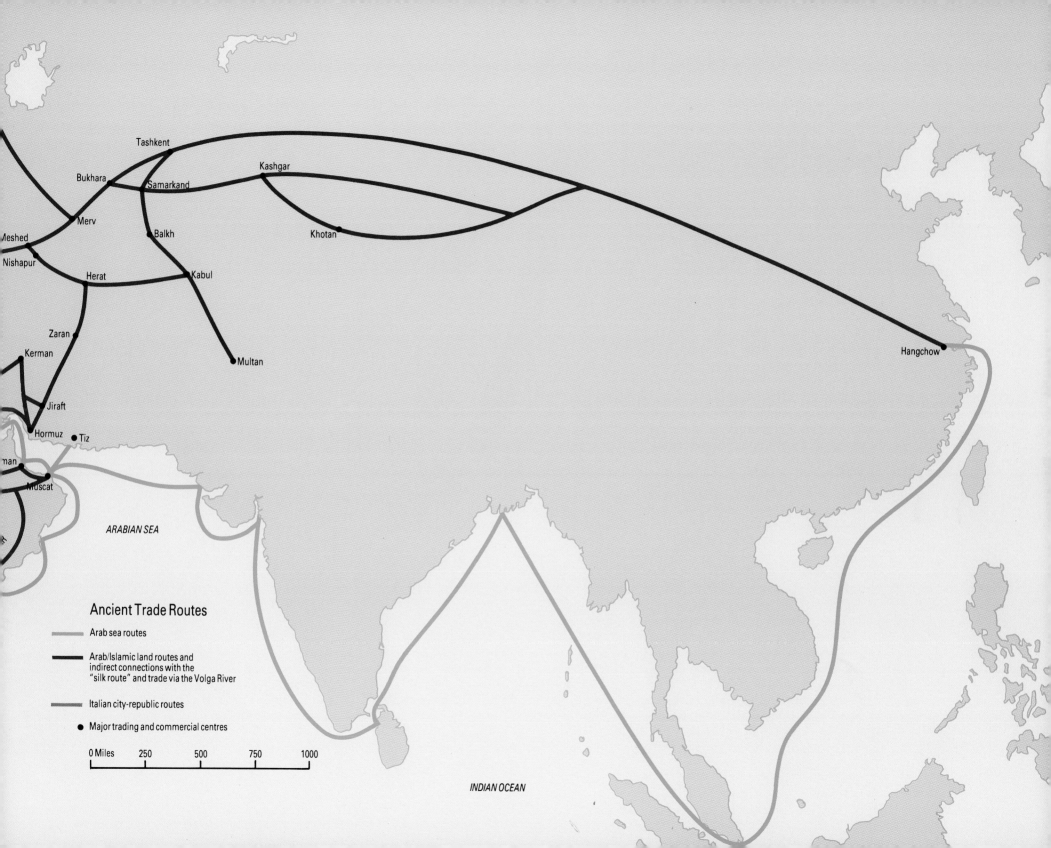

Ancient Trade Routes

Tashkent

Bukhara

Samarkand

Kashgar

Merv

Balkh

Khotan

Meshed

Nishapur

Herat

Kabul

Zaran

Multan

Kerman

Jiraft

Hormuz

Tiz

man

Muscat

Hangchow

ARABIAN SEA

Arab sea routes

Arab/Islamic land routes and
indirect connections with the
"silk route" and trade via the Volga River

Italian city-republic routes

● Major trading and commercial centres

0 Miles   250   500   750   1000

INDIAN OCEAN

EGYPTIAN

The Egyptians favoured multiple pendant ornaments; metal surfaces richly decorated with applied filigree and granulation; an abundant use of turquoise, carnelian, faience and glass; colourful beads strung or pendant; and multi-coloured combinations of stones set on thin sheets of beaten gold. All are characteristic of Bedouin jewellery.

The Egyptians commonly embellished plain or engraved metal surfaces with relief decorations, known as "applied" filigree, and granulation – both techniques also popular with today's Arabian Bedouin craftsmen.

The Bedouin of Central Arabia also echo the Egyptians' love of turquoise whose use of this semi-precious stone is of remote antiquity; Egyptian turquoise scarab beetle-shapes were found in the tombs of the Pharaohs. Among the Bedouin it appears occasionally as a silver pendant.

Most ancient Egyptian jewellery had magical significance, so much so that it is almost impossible for scholars to distinguish amuletic from purely ornamental especially since the Egyptians took their everyday jewellery with them to the grave. They believed that green feldspar and turquoise were the colour of new life; red carnelian, the colour of life-blood; and blue lapis lazuli, the colour of the heavens. For them the cowrie shell and fish shapes gave protection; and the scarab shape was a potent amulet.

The scarab is a dung beetle, revered as the symbol of regeneration. The coiled snake was also a popular jewellery motif which had amuletic significance for the Egyptians. The Peninsular people may

Above: an Egyptian necklace of the Eleventh Dynasty, about 2020 BC, resembling a broad collar. All the beads, the two semi-circular terminals, and seven

mummiform pendants are of glazed composition, either blue, white or purplish in colour.

have inherited the shape from the Egyptians, developing it into the coiled snake-like bracelets worn by the Arabian Bedouin today.

The earliest Egyptian necklaces were simple strands of beads, but later in the Middle Kingdom – the zenith of the art of the Egyptian jeweller – gold-working in every technique was performed.

The New Kingdom saw the use of imitation gems become more common and broad collar necklaces became greatly varied. After the New Kingdom ended, Egyptian jewellery for the most part exhibited Hellenistic and Roman characteristics and the many rings and earrings emerged which Bedouin ornaments resemble so closely.

AFRICAN

Considering the proximity of Africa to Arabia, and the ancient Arab trade route connection, quite apart from the shared Islamic faith which involves annual pilgrimage of African Muslims to Mecca, it is not surprising that Arabian Bedouin silver jewellery occasionally exhibits African characteristics.

The chunky anklets depicted here are similar to African ornaments. Such large ornaments were once fashionable with the Ashanti of Africa who lived in part of modern day Ghana. Although of similar bold design, Ashanti jewellery was mostly fashioned in gold, and at Benin, capital of a southern Nigerian Kingdom on the west coast, superb gold work was accomplished by the *cire perdue* [lost wax] process in the late fifteenth and sixteenth centuries – a technique not used on the Arabian Peninsula. Jewellery from the African continent is fashioned in brass, iron and tin as well as gold and silver.

Just when African influence upon Arabian Bedouin body ornament began is impossible to ascertain. It is an influence that is less emphatic than others, for much African jewellery is grotesque in that it is enormous in size and designed to distort the natural shape of the body.

A silversmith from the African continent may have been responsible for the manufacture of these cumbersome anklets, which, although found in Saudi Arabia, closely resemble African jewellery. Many pilgrims who were artisans have remained on the Peninsula after completing the Hajj. Jewellery as a negotiable asset is often sold to provide funds to complete the pilgrimage. They are, in fact, claimed as locally manufactured. Anklets, known as khalkhal [plural, khalakhil], such as those shown here are sometimes worn as armlets, zand [plural, zunud]. A heavy anklet or armlet usually weighs approximately 200 grammes. The silver content in these ornaments appears to be low, and possibly tin is the base metal alloyed for they look quite dull. The design is geometric and has been carried out by engraving for the lines and chasing for the other relief.

خلخال (جمع خلاخيل)   *khalkhal (pl. khalakhil)*

زند (جمع زنود)   *zand (pl. zunud)*

ORIENTAL

The link between the Far East and Arabia is often visible in traditional Peninsular jewellery.

Several ornate and exotic-looking pieces found in the Arabian Peninsula Bedouin range look distinctly Far Eastern and may be the result of influence felt when the ancient trade routes flourished, or later, during the spread of Islam.

The features that may have exotic origins are: the inclusion of tiny objects in hollow jewellery to rattle in time with a dancer's movements: the bell shape, which appears occasionally as pendants in Bedouin jewellery; lavish use of relief ornamentation – a laborious technique often used to build up a domed surface in an elaborate manner and seen in some Bedouin bracelets.

Though sometimes reminiscent of Bedouin jewellery, Bhutanese and Nepalese jewellery are distinctive in that they favour high-relief ornamentation often set with turquoise. Their jewellery is more closely related to Tibet than to their other neighbour, India.

The Tibetans are very different from their principal neighbours, the Chinese and the Indians. Much of their jewellery is devotional. The effect of Tibetan jewellery is achieved by an interplay of predominant turquoise encrustation, sometimes forming elaborate patterns with an abundance of false granulation, pearled wire and coarse beaded borders used for decorative accent. In this and the lavish turquoise, mounted in high relief, affinity with Bedouin buttons and beads may be seen.

The Chinese, too, have used turquoise

lavishly in their jewellery for thousands of years, and their ornamentation of the third and fifth centuries AD also shows granulation in triangular borders enhanced further by three minute granules, again forming a triangle – exactly the same pattern as granulated decoration in Arabian jewellery. It is thought that the art of granulation

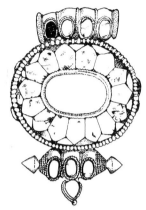

Left: *a Tibetan amulet box, eighteenth century* AD. *The metal is gold and the stones are turquoise. It was worn on the pigtail of an official's servant.*

Below: *These bracelets could have come from Nepal, Bhutan or Tibet, but are Bedouin.*

probably reached the Chinese from the West. Granulated decoration in diamond patterns was in use on the Arabian Peninsula as early as the first century AD. This points to an active link between China and Arabia and reminds one of the vast distances covered by the ancient sea and land trade routes. See map pages 46/47.

It has been established that the nomadic

Scythians and Russians exerted some influence on Chinese jewellery. Characteristic of Scythian ornamentation was the incorporation of stylistic animal shapes into jewellery, a fashion found over a long period of time and vast geographical area from Europe to China. The featured terminal ends in Bedouin jewellery may have evolved from this style.

PERSIAN

Persian influence on Arabian Bedouin jewellery is probably the strongest single outside influence, especially in the north, south and east of the Peninsula, for the Persians interacted closely with the pre-Islamic Bedouin Arabs from these areas.

Studies of ancient Persian body ornament are usually based on the Oxus River Treasure found in 1877, the history of which is unfortunately obscure. It may represent an accumulation of two or more centuries of treasure, and was probably hidden about 330 BC when Alexander the Great's Greek army was advancing.

Greek historians have written of the remarkable quantities of gold worn by the Persians in a variety of forms: bracelets, torques and appliquéd ornaments.

The Pheonicians were dominated by the Persians from 539 to 332 BC and Pheonician influence was profound upon the jewellery crafted at the time. Yet it can be observed that Persian jewellery tends to be technically simpler than Phoenician, although the former's lavish use of gold gives it singular opulence.

Persian jewellery also displays characteristics inherited from Mesopotamia and neighbouring Elam, which appear to include influences of the Central Asian nomadic Scythians. The artistic vitality of the Persians has continued since the conquest of their Empire by Alexander, throughout the rise and fall of subsequent civilizations.

Its influence on Bedouin jewellery is unmistakable: multiple choker necklaces of an elegance rarely matched, pendanted bells and hooped bracelets with bulbous terminal ends, which suggest the stylized

One of a pair of gold armlets found as part of the Oxus Treasure, Persian Empire, about fifth–fourth century BC.

animal heads so popular with the Persians. The advent of Islam may have been responsible for the simplication of this animal shape for bracelet terminals, but this cannot be proved conclusively owing to the lack of old jewellery.

PHOENICIAN

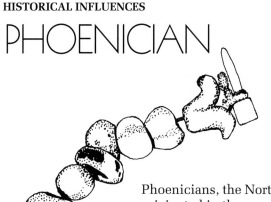

This necklace is dated circa seventh–sixth century BC and was found at Tharros, Sardinia. It comprises glass beads and gold pendants, the central pendant depicting cobras and a beetle-shaped motif, probably a divine symbol.

Phoenicians, the Northern Canaanites who originated in the area that is now Lebanon and the coast of Syria, were at one time the greatest seafaring traders of the ancient world. As both traders and colonists, the Phoenicians in the first century BC were responsible for carrying the jewellery of Western Asia through to the Mediterranean. They were also famed for their skill in glass-making and their jewellery-making techniques.

The Phoenicians are often credited with the invention of glass but this medium had been known since the mid-second millennium BC. According to tradition, however, glass was accidentally discovered when a group of ship-wrecked Phoenician sailors lit a fire on a sandy beach. Colourful glass necklaces were a popular Phoenician adornment; their irregular-sized, multi-coloured, stranded beads with pendants at regular intervals are very similar in construction to those worn by the Arabian Bedouin.

Phoenician ornamentation included amuletic motifs derived from Egyptian jewellery, yet the patterns often being so transformed in shape and combination of shapes that they would not have been recognized even by contemporary Egyptians. During their years of seafaring service to successive masters – Egyptians, Mesopotamians, Persians, Greeks and Romans – the influence of this vigorous race upon the development of body ornament was profound and far-reaching, From the eighth to the fourth centuries BC, the Phoenicians became dominated by the various empires situated to the East in Mesopotamia and Elam, until eventually they were defeated by Rome in the third and second centuries BC.

CELTIC

Celtic jewellery of the first century BC, found in England and France, includes the torque or neck-ring regarded as the principal item in Celtic jewellery, and matching bracelets of twisted rods forming hoops which are astonishingly similar to Arabian Bedouin counterparts.

Surprisingly these wrought hoops are held to be Central Arabian in conception. The possible carriers of influence for this style may have been the seafaring Phoenicians. Trade between the Middle East and the Western Celts had been long established by them. To further their commerce, they set up trading posts which became colonies [such as Marseilles in what is now France]. They sailed as far as the Baltic Sea and the West Coast of Africa, trading in tin from England, silver from Spain, fur from the Baltic Sea area, gold and ivory from Central Africa, linen and glassware from Egypt, and perfumes and spices from Arabia, no doubt carrying jewellery among their cargo.

It is known that the arable segment of land which stretches across the top of Arabia from the Gulf of Aqaba, sweeping upward to the Mediterranean and beyond the eastern valleys of the Tigris and Euphrates rivers (commonly known as the Fertile Crescent) was once the site of flourishing Middle Eastern civilizations. It can be seen why its position seemed to keep the Arabian Peninsula's own centres of civilization geographically captive. It is recorded that the Peninsula civilizations "absorbed" the culture of their Fertile Crescent neighbours; yet whilst cross-influence and migration are established

A first century BC, South British Late Iron Age, torque, or neck-ring, found on Ken Hill, Snettisham, Norfolk, England. The hollow ring terminals are ornamented in relief and with chased hatching and lines and dots, and crimped ridges; the terminals are soldered on to ends of hoop which comprises eight strands twisted together, each strand consisting of eight wires twisted together. The bracelets shown on page 79 bear striking similarity to this torque.

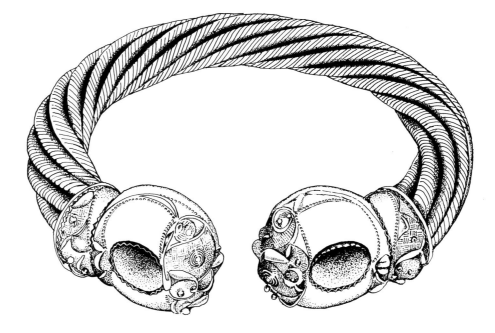

facts, the jewellery of the Arabian Bedouin, as one small facet of Peninsula culture, does seem to indicate some individual evolvement.

Investigation shows positive links in the chain of Arabia's jewellery history do exist. For example, the traditional mace-shaped terminal bead of so many of today's Bedouin necklaces is identical to that found (in 1952) in the tomb at Jawan, eastern Saudi Arabia, which can be dated about 100 AD – though the Jawan terminal bead is of gold and today's terminal beads are of silver. And the self-same shape of bead, in the same position, occurs (also in gold) in the necklaces of the Greeks of the fourth century BC. Another Jawan bead was cowrie-shaped – a design it shares with the beads of Egyptian necklaces of the Middle Kingdom, dating from about 1900 to 1500 BC. The cowrie shell itself was favoured as adornment as long ago as 5000 BC, during the Halaf period of neighbouring Iraq: the shells came from the Red Sea and the Arabian Gulf.

53

GREEK

three centuries of great poverty, which produced very little jewellery.

The Greeks eventually became highly skilled jewellers, but used little colour in the form of gemstones. Instead, their craftsmen employed decorative techniques to embellish plain metal surfaces, especially granulation. Although jewellery from the Pyramids attests to Egyptian use of this technique, it is the early Greeks who are credited with developing it. In either case, it is likely that the Arabian use of this form of decoration came from Egypt, and that any refinement of its use came much later from the Greeks and Etruscans, brought to the Peninsula through the Graeco-Roman amalgam in the Byzantine Empire.

The first engraved stones appeared during this period and the Greeks became the finest gem engravers of the ancient world. The end of this period, fifth and fourth centuries BC, produced high quality Greek jewellery, and elaborate necklaces made their appearance.

The Hellenistic Age, beginning with the conquests by Alexander in the late third century BC, transformed the Greek world and the former Persian Empire, the latter being Hellenized by Greek settlement: and the Greeks in turn were exposed to the newly conquered Egyptian and western Asian civilizations. It can be said to have ended with the inauguration of the Roman Empire in 27 BC.

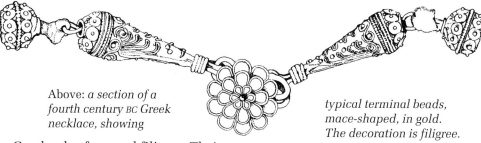

Above: *a section of a fourth century BC Greek necklace, showing* *typical terminal beads, mace-shaped, in gold. The decoration is filigree.*

Above: *a pair of eighth century BC gold earrings. The discs exhibit fine granulation surrounding a collet.*

From the back springs a curved "stalk" on the end of which is an inlaid finial, or capping.

The early period of Greek jewellery, 850–700 BC, demonstrated the higheststandards of workmanship. It is probable that the famed goldsmiths from Phoenicia set up workshops and taught the secrets of their trade to Greek apprentices, because the Greeks had previously suffered two or

The Greeks also favoured filigree. Their application of these decorative techniques, and particularly the use of pendanted bells appearing on Greek necklaces in the seventh century, are similar to Bedouin jewellery.

In the Classical Greek period, 600–475 BC, jewellery was again rare at first but became more plentiful after the Persian Wars. Colourful gems were rarely used, however, and filigree became increasingly popular; the work was less fine than before the Persian Wars.

During this period massive finger-rings with stones wider than a single finger became fashionable, a style also seen in the Bedouin finger-ring range. It is interesting that, among the new jewellery motifs of the Hellenistic Age, the crescent shape made its appearance, introduced to Greece originally in the eighth and seventh centuries from western Asia, where, as a symbol of the Moon God, it had had amuletic significance in remote antiquity.

54

ETRUSCAN

The Etruscans, a race of uncertain origin, came to Italy in the ninth century BC establishing themselves in what is now Tuscany and creating a civilization which flourished in the northern area of the Italian Isthmus from about 700 BC. They reached the height of their power between the sixth and fifth centuries BC, declining in the fourth century BC, but continuing to the middle of the second century BC, until eventually absorbed by Rome.

Early Etruscan jewellery, sixth to fourth century BC, was characterized by its abundance, its technical perfection and its variety. Etruscans loved colour and used beautiful Phoenician glass and faience in their jewellery with excellent effect. The technical knowledge of jewellery-making reached them from the Phoenicians, but they themselves perfected the various techniques. The Etruscans became the most brilliant jewellery craftsmen of this Classical Age and their workmanship achieved a height of excellence never before equalled. As the greatest experts in the technique of granulation, it is commonly held that this skill has never been satisfactorily imitated.

The late Etruscan period, 40–250 BC, brought forth ornaments fashioned from sheet gold, often convex, with simple embossing combined with filigree and granulation for decorative accent. The Arabian Bedouin wear a forehead ornament which echoes these Etruscan jewellery characteristics. Gradually, the Etruscans were drawn into the Greek cultural orbit and they adopted Hellenistic fashions, where filigree largely replaced granulation for relief decoration.

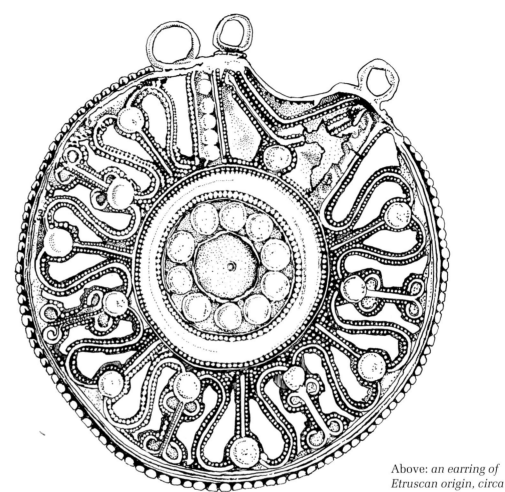

The scarab beetle shape was a popular jewellery motif with the Etruscans, which they may have adopted from the seafaring Phoenicians, who had in turn taken it from Egypt, where it was a symbol of regeneration. For the Etruscans it also signified resurrection and immortality, although the Phoenicians considered it merely ornamental. This may provide a clue to their origin.

Above: *an earring of Etruscan origin, circa 700-500 BC shows the technical brilliance characteristic of their work. The open-work opus interassile" has been pierced out with a chisel and the decoration achieved with repoussé and granulation. The central collet was once inlaid.*

ROMAN

The Romans were indebted to the Greeks for their jewellery. With the inauguration of the Roman Empire in 27 BC, the former austere Roman appearance gave way to the wearing of fabulous jewellery, which was at first merely a continuation of Hellenic styles. Yet despite the considerable impact of the Greek jewellery craft it was the Romans who perfected several jewellery-making techniques, such as wire-making. And, whilst the Greeks, as we have seen, were considered the first and finest gem engravers of the ancient world, the Romans were responsible for fantastic designs in gem engraving. During the Roman period great efforts were made for the subject of an engraving to correspond to the colour of the gem engraved: cows grazed on green jasper, the "slaying of Marsyas" was executed on red carnelian, marine deities were cut into aquamarine and harvest scenes appeared on nothing but golden-coloured gemstones.

Massive finger-rings, popularized by the Greeks, became fashionable with the Romans and also in this era several rings were worn at once, one on each finger. And, sometimes the Romans also wore several slender rings each set with a different stone, uniting into one, but generally a single intaglio formed the bezel. Invariably Roman rings exhibited elaborate tapered shoulders which were often carved – all characteristics and fashions favoured in the wearing of Bedouin finger-rings in Arabia today.

Betrothal rings first appeared in Roman times and have continued to be a symbol of marriage ever since, although the forms of these rings have varied greatly over the centuries. The plain bands of today bear no resemblance to the betrothal rings of the past, and it seems that they made their appearance as late as early this century. Plain bands were worn on the "wedding" finger prior to this, but they were known as "keeper" rings, being placed on that finger just for the function of keeping the other ring or rings safely in place. Although the Arabian Bedouin do not have a betrothal ring as such, jewellery as dowry upon marriage does include finger-rings. Modern Arabians now follow the "betrothal" ring tradition begun by the ancient Romans.

The snake motif, which had amuletic significance for the Egyptians, was worn by the Greeks and continued to be popular with the Romans, a fashion persisting in jewellery of the Western world. Possibly the snake-like coils which appear as Bedouin bracelets today were derived from the Romans but the influence may have come from ancient Egypt. The snake certainly had symbolic significance very early in the Arabian Gulf, as evidenced by the discovery of the remains of snakes in sacred burials under the floors of excavated dwellings on Bahrain, the site of ancient Dilmun. Geoffrey Bibby, a noted English archaeologist working with a Danish expedition, wrote in his book *Looking For Dilmun*, that these snakes, which were generally accompanied by a pearl or blue bead, appeared to be buried beneath houses of the Dilmun Civilization in order to protect the occupants.

Right: *A first century AD Roman bracelet, fashioned in gold in the form of a coiled snake. It was found at Pompeii and given by the King of Naples to Sir William Hamilton; later in the possession of Viscount Dillon.*

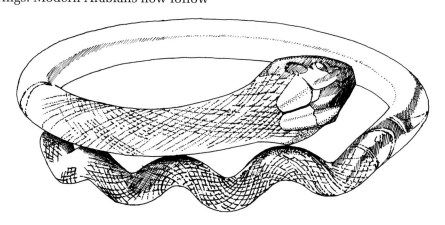

BYZANTINE

From the Byzantine Empire – an amalgam of Greek, Roman and Eastern cultures – the Golden Age of Islam inherited jewellery-making techniques and styles. Constantine, Roman Emperor from 324 to 337 AD, made Christianity the official religion of the Empire, and established a magnificent new city as centre of the eastern half of the Roman Empire on the site of the old Greek town of Byzantium, calling it Constantinople – "Constantine's city". After the fall of Rome in the following century, Byzantium/ Constantinople became the capital of the remaining eastern portion of the Roman Empire. Upon Byzantium and its Emperors, the cultural influences were focused, and Byzantium became the centre of innovation in style of bodily ornament.

Greek culture was joined by Roman in Byzantium and techniques developed under Roman rule persisted into Byzantine Christendom, and thence into Islam, although for the most part in territory outside Arabia.

Earrings revealing their Byzantine derivation: both the penannular wire hoop style with filigree cage attached, and the crescent-shaped style, are worn by Arabian Bedouin women today.

The extensive use of wire in jewellery became prevalent with the early Christians and Byzantines, as did a variety of chains and clasps, which became immensely popular in Medieval Europe. Bedouin jewellery from Arabia includes various chains, constructed with many different types of links, spacers and baubles combining several crafting techniques.

This pair of Byzantine earrings, dated about 600 AD, are reported to have been found at Lambousa, Cyprus. Lambousa was the find-spot of the two famous Byzantine silver hoards, known respectively as the first and second Cyprus Treasures, which are now divided between the British Museum, the Metropolitan Museum of Art, New York, and the Cyprus Museum, Nicosia. The treasures were found before the First World War.

These "opus interassile", or chiselled openwork not sawed, earrings have been decorated with chasing in a floral scroll pattern, the border being of beaded wire. This crescent shape is typical of Byzantine work.

The plainer types of Bedouin chain, a series of simple connections without decorative pretension, seem to be the natural evolvement of the earliest use of wire in jewellery: but one particular intricate rope-like chain in plaited herringbone style used for the *jnad*, an enormous Bedouin ornament which is worn round the neck and under one arm, is identical to chains found in Early Christian jewellery from Carthage, North Africa, dated 400 AD, and appears again in Byzantine jewellery of 600 AD.
Arabian Bedouin *jnad*: see page 81.

The great Byzantine Empire thrived for over a thousand years until Constantinople fell to the Ottoman Turks in 1453, to be later renamed Istanbul. In this way, earlier expressions in decorative art flowed into the Ottoman Empire and onward to the Islamic world.

جناد *jnad*

57

ISLAMIC & CRUSADER

Following the dawn of Islam in the seventh century AD, and the subsequent spread of the faith through the former Byzantine Empire, Iraq, Persia, Egypt and North Africa, Spain and east towards China, body ornament in these areas was subject to many influences. Thus it is remarkable that Arabian Bedouin jewellery has emerged so little altered.

The crescent shape, *hilal*, a popular jewellery motif with the Byzantines, and the emblem of the Turkish sultans, became the symbol of Islam and is now displayed above the mosques throughout the world. It represents the waxing of the moon between new moon and full and heralds each new month of the "Hijrah", the Islamic year. The crescent remains a

most popular motif in Middle Eastern jewellery. Other moon shapes became popular too: the half and the full moon, *bader*. The latter was romanticized by the great poets of the Classical Age of Islam, and according to their verses, a full moon heralds a night for lovers. The inclusion of religious amulets as part of Islamic jewellery also emanated from the new religion; these were often worn as pendants which were inscribed with the name of Allah. Other amulets took the form of charm cases which contained Koranic verses.

Several centuries later, another major event occurred in world history which may have affected Middle Eastern jewellery styles. In 1096, prince, peasant and priest marched out of Europe to wage a holy war, the first of the series of "Crusades", an epic struggle between Christian and Muslim for a land sacred to both. These Crusades, which ended in 1291, were responsible for bringing influence to bear upon Middle Eastern civilization and culture.

The Crusaders are vividly remembered today for their protective garb, the heavy chain mail, which may well have influenced the Islamic silversmiths of the period. It is a source of wonderment to see Arabian Bedouin in meshed collar necklaces made of interlinking rings, bells and shapes which may have been inspired by the chain mail worn by the Crusaders. It is also interesting to speculate upon the possibility that the Crusaders were in some measure responsible for the popularity of chains as jewellery.

Above: *This meshed pectoral* [kirdan] *resembles chain mail. Possibly the first smith to make it was inspired by the armour of the Crusaders. The cloth backing is missing. In Yemen, such pectorals were given to the bride by her father.*

MODERN

The Hejaz, north-west Arabia, as the main entry point for foreign pilgrims to the holy cities of Mecca and Medina, has undoubtedly been an important source of foreign influence upon locally manufactured jewellery. It has also been the main route in the past by which non-Arabian silver ornaments entered the Peninsula. Whilst most of the Bedouin silver jewellery found in Arabia has been crafted on the Peninsula, occasionally a piece is identified as work from another Middle Eastern country, attesting to the mobility of this dowry jewellery in the possession of a Bedouin wife.

The recent trend in Arabian body ornament is towards light-weight mass-produced gold jewellery which is not traditional, although some design characteristics of traditional Bedouin jewellery do appear, such as the crescent shape and multiple pendants.

These elaborate, delicate-looking gold trinkets have flooded the Arabian jewellery *suqs* come from India, Pakistan, Syria and Lebanon, and recently craftsmen from these countries have begun to work in Arabia. Shown here, right, is a typical jewellery shop display of the gold ornaments which are often set with glass, or pink corundum which is sold as ruby. All over the world, at present, jewellery shops sell pink corundum as ruby when, according to the rules agreed to by gemologists, corundum is correctly classified as sapphire, unless it is red in colour, when it is termed a ruby. The point at which corundum ceases to be pink sapphire, and becomes a red ruby should be assessed by a gemologist.

The preference for this modern gold jewellery is clearly not just a matter of gold versus silver, as discussed in Chapter Five, for now Arabian Bedouin women are beginning to appreciate ornaments of lighter weight than the traditional cumbersome styles, especially in the case of nose ornaments. It could be said that this gold jewellery symbolizes the new affluent phase in Arabia's history, just as the passing of the traditional silver jewellery marks the end of the era of obscurity.

A Riyadh shop showing mass-produced jewellery from India, Pakistan, Lebanon and Syria. Craftsmen from these countries are now producing this jewellery on the Arabian Peninsula also.

59

REGIONAL STYLES

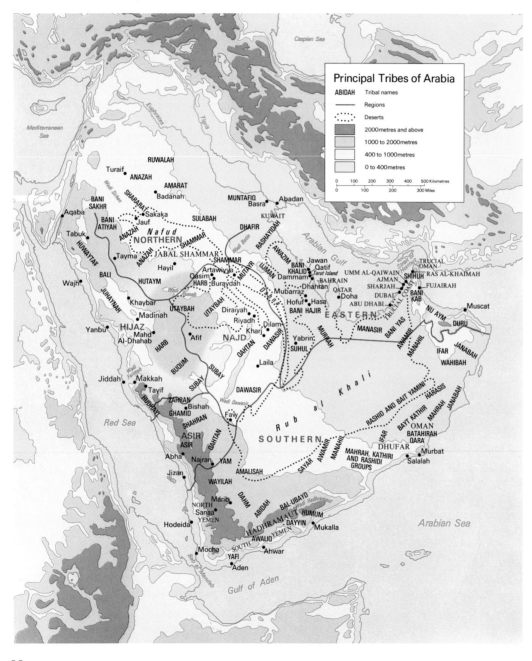

Principal Tribes of Arabia

ABIDAH   Tribal names
———   Regions
·······   Deserts

2000metres and above
1000 to 2000metres
400 to 1000metres
0 to 400metres

The various sources consulted about Arabian regional styles in Bedouin jewellery often provided conflicting details. This is to be expected, since the nomadic life of the Bedouin, particularly in recent decades with the advent of wheeled transport, brings him into frequent contact with itinerant traders, silversmiths and other Bedouin. It is known that regional styles did exist prior to the unification of the tribes earlier this century, as a result of limited contact with neighbours and with influences from directly outside the Peninsula. Now, with few exceptions, it seems that the same basic characteristics are shared by all the widely separated areas in Arabia, while the oldest intact examples of Bedouin silver jewellery confirm regional individuality.

North-east Arabia

North of the Najd, Central Arabia, is the district of the Northern Frontiers, the neighbouring countries being west to east: Jordan, Iraq and Kuwait, beyond which lies Iran – Persia of old. It is therefore not surprising that the oldest available pieces of Bedouin silver jewellery from north-east Arabia strongly resemble the ornaments of the Persians. Torque-like choker necklaces, *kirdala*, supporting multiple pendants of elongated beads, and hoop bracelets with featured terminals, are two examples of jewellery which suggest Persian influence, and are claimed to come from that region.

It is also claimed that the small, gem-encrusted triangular pendants with chains, which often support the silver scarab or pistachio motif pendants, rather than the more common bell, are also from that area. The scarab motif and gem-encrusted surfaces suggest Egyptian influence so, logically, these would seem to come from there, since the influence of ancient Egypt would have been felt most in the north of the Peninsula. Moreover, strands of coloured glass beads are supposed to have been popular in the North, a distant echo from ancient trade route traffic.

Eastern Province

The Eastern Province is the region along the Arabian Gulf which was once called Al Hasa, after the "murmuring" of the waters of the large oasis in which the former capital, Hofuf, lies. Again, the hollow hooped bracelets with featured hollow terminals resembling Persian bracelets [matched pairs worn on each wrist] occur as in the north-east of Arabia.

This region was occupied by the Ottoman Turks from 1871 until 1913, which may account for the crescent moon shape, the emblem of the Turkish Sultans, being somewhat more prevalent here.

The bulbous bead and hooped earrings, claimed to be typical of the Eastern Province, do not suggest any specific origin, but the heavy spiked bracelets and anklets resemble African jewellery. Both of these styles probably arrived by way of trading ships, which entered the Arabian Gulf. Gold-washed, linked, plate-like head ornaments are also part of Eastern Arabian traditional jewellery, and similar to Indian west-coast tribal ornaments.

Western Province

The Hejaz, the region adjacent to the Red Sea, which includes Jiddah and the Holy Cities of Makkah and Madinah, has been exposed to many outside influences from trading ships and the annual flow of pilgrims. The most characteristic piece of jewellery from this area is the half-moon style of earring and nose-ring, which is also worn in North African countries. An unusual bead common to Hejazi and North African tribal jewellery is fish-shaped, the *samak*.

Central Arabia

The Central Province, the Najd, comprises a large part of the interior and contains the capital city, Riyadh.

The twisted "Celtic" style hooped bracelets are said to be from Central Arabia, as is a beautiful head ornament, which is made up of two elaborately decorated plates placed each side of the head, with the many-stranded connecting chains worn draped over the tresses at the back of the head.

Heavy twisted metal was popular with Roman and Celtic jewellery, whilst chains as adornment were fashionable in Medieval times. The early trade with the Romans, and later with the Crusaders, may have been responsible for bringing these styles to the Najd.

Marami, the thin silver finger-rings worn in groups of two, three or four are supposed to have originated in the Wadi Dawasir area in the Central Province, although these are also common in the

neighbouring southern regions. The most distinctive difference is the use of turquoise and fine gold in the heartland of Arabia.

The South

South of the Hejaz, or Western Province, are the three districts of Tihamah, Asir and Najran, often called the Asir.

Bells and belled ornaments are said to have originated in Najran. The intricately hinged-opening and pinned-fastening variety of anklet, bracelet and belt are characteristic of the Asir and also of neighbouring Yemen. From this area, and Yemen also, come the elaborate meshed collars, *kirdan*, which resemble the chain mail of the Crusaders.

The origin of the design of the flower-like ring and other large stoned rings is claimed by the Asir and the Hotat Bani Tamim people in West-Central Arabia. These are worn on the middle and fore-fingers of both hands, whilst the slim rings, *marami*, are usually worn on other fingers.

The number and positioning of rings varies throughout the Peninsula and on special occasions a Bedouin woman will wear as many rings as she possesses.

Red and brownish-red stones are commonly set in south-western jewellery and ornaments. The semi-precious stones are carnelian and strung beads are usually agate and coral, real and fake.

كردله   *kirdala*

مرامي   *marami*

كردان   *kirdan*

4 TECHNIQUES

MASS PRODUCTION methods cannot successfully copy most pieces of Bedouin jewellery, due to the detail which can only be achieved by the skilled hands of the craftsman. The styles, decoration, and basic techniques of fashioning jewellery, unchanged since ancient times, are followed by Bedouin jewellers in an age

A silversmith sits cross-legged fashioning metal into ornaments.

Today many of the artisans are retiring and the younger generation turning to more profitable occupations.

when hand-made items are eagerly sought. This revived appreciation in the Western world for hand-crafted objects is one expression of modern man's emerging desire to return to a simpler life close to nature.

The Bedouin favour traditional styles of jewellery for being decorative, valuable and useful. The workmanship naturally varies from smith to smith, but the silver content is becoming increasingly low. Fake gems are more often incorporated than real ones, although it has long been the custom for a proportion of cheaper jewellery to be manufactured albeit fashioned in identical traditional designs.

Whatever the metal content, the techniques employed for fashioning the jewellery are the same. Annealing and hammering are the initial processes which are followed by cutting in readiness for embossing, repoussé, chasing and engraving – all methods of giving relief to flat surfaces. The ornamental techniques of filigree and granulation add yet another dimension. Wire of even gauge is produced for making chains; yet other techniques exist whereby metal can be wrought, cast, fused and soldered. For an elaborate ornament a combination of these techniques is employed; but sometimes only one decorative technique is used alone, liberally, for an exotic effect.

The silversmith

The Bedouin silversmith is usually born into the artisan class and his craft is generally passed on to him by his father, who instructs his son in traditional jewellery-making techniques and encourages him to produce the styles traditionally favoured in his area.

Silversmiths in Arabia are mostly settled or semi-settled folk concentrated at the oases and coastal towns, but they are occasionally nomadic when affiliated with a large tribe, for whose needs they cater for an indefinite period. Often drawn from a town, the silversmith would become part of the tribal structure, although considered ignoble because of his artisan class.

The settled silversmiths are generally found working close to the *suqs*, where they sit cross-legged, singly or in small groups tapping out their silver on an anvil, often bare to the waist because of the heat of a desert climate intensified by the fire over which they work the metal.

Traditional styles are favoured for jewellery, silver dagger handles and scabbards, but occasionally an item of Bedouin jewellery displays originality; for example: in the pistachio nut-shaped pendant. Such an unusual ornament proves the theory of an original idea conceived by an individualistic craftsman. Most of the jewellery he produces will be characterized by symbolic shapes and abstract, often intricate, designs in geometrical and floral motifs.

It is evident that "arabesque", the Islamic form of decoration, has greatly influenced the Bedouin jeweller. Zahi Khuri writes: "Primitive forms of arabesque existed in pre-Islamic times and were borrowed by the Greeks and Romans, but the richness and most exquisite renderings of this style were only achieved by Muslim designers. Essentially, it is a linear ornament, an interlaced pattern based either on pure geometric relations with a variety of angular movements, or on endlessly flowing, curvilinears, sometimes displaying leaf, flower and animal motifs.

It is the strength and harmony of their linear designs and their mathematical lucidity that has made them unique and outstanding among other styles of art. It is no accident that Muslim artists adopted this style and developed out of it some of the greatest patterns ever recorded in the history of art."

The simple life in Arabia during the early days of Islam manifested itself in the way the Arabs lived in their houses. The only important piece of furniture was the elaborate chest in which clothes and linen were kept. To the Arabs of this early Islamic period, the beauty of the house was expressed by the surfaces that made it; its floor, walls and roof. Much attention was therefore devoted to the decoration of these surfaces.

Different motifs, mainly abstract, were developed and utilized to decorate flat surfaces. The development of arabesques was further encouraged by the early Muslim's aversion to the representation of human beings. Consequently Muslim calligraphers utilized their talent in copying the Koran and produced the richest of abstract motifs that human imagination can possibly conceive. Since then Koranic verses and the Kufic script have been blended so magnificently that they have become almost inseparable.

Arabesques are also executed on stone,

63

TOOLS OF THE TRADE

pottery, glass, bronze and wood. Bedouin jewellery is undoubtedly another medium through which the designs and decoration of arabesques can be expressed.

The metal-working trades have suffered severely from the competition of imports and rising costs of labour and materials in recent years, and many craftsmen have gradually been forced into performing metal repairwork. Many others are retiring and the younger generation is turning to more profitable occupations, so that the traditional style of ornament is becoming increasingly rare. Many Bedouin are being absorbed into new industries, developed during the present economic boom, and the younger generation are leaving their desert homes for the opportunities in the cities. The inevitable result of these planned or impulsive changes in the lifestyle of the Bedouin, mean that the long, low, black tents glimpsed between the dunes will soon vanish like a mirage, along with their inhabitants' colourful way of life, their fascinating garments and beautiful silver jewellery.

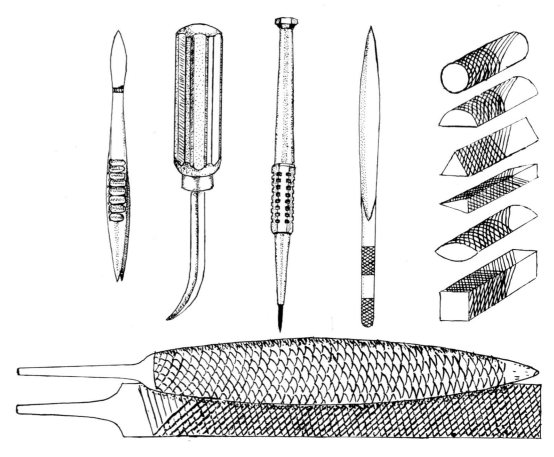

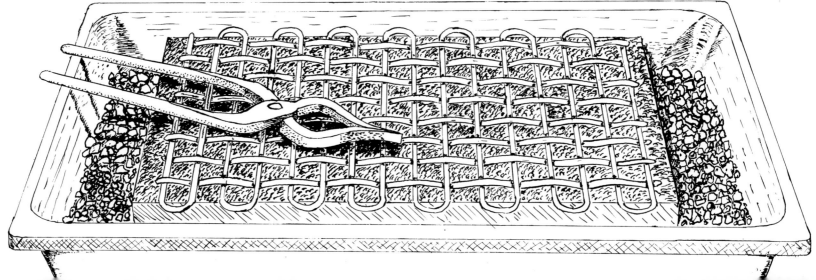

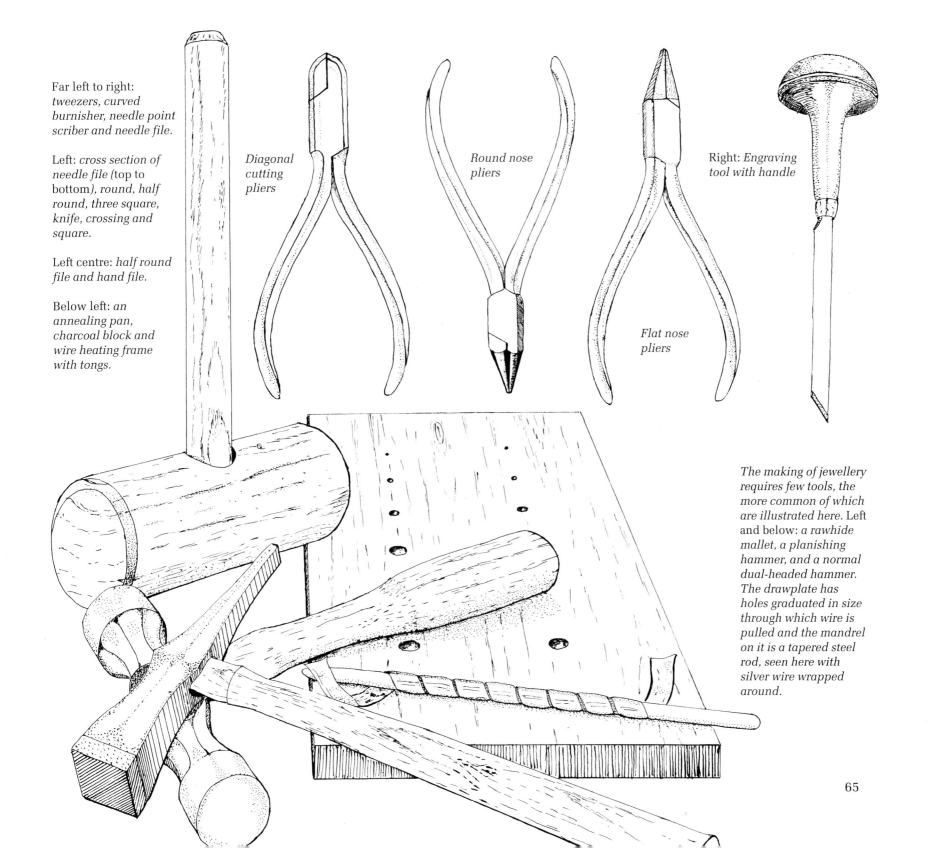

Far left to right: *tweezers, curved burnisher, needle point scriber and needle file.*

Left: *cross section of needle file (top to bottom), round, half round, three square, knife, crossing and square.*

Left centre: *half round file and hand file.*

Below left: *an annealing pan, charcoal block and wire heating frame with tongs.*

Diagonal cutting pliers

Round nose pliers

Flat nose pliers

Right: *Engraving tool with handle*

The making of jewellery requires few tools, the more common of which are illustrated here. Left and below: *a rawhide mallet, a planishing hammer, and a normal dual-headed hammer. The drawplate has holes graduated in size through which wire is pulled and the mandrel on it is a tapered steel rod, seen here with silver wire wrapped around.*

65

ANNEALING & HAMMERING

تحمية وطرق

تحمية	*tahmiyah*
طرق	*tarq*
حفر	*hafr*
أساور	*asawir*

Annealing [*tahmiyah*] is the first process in fashioning metal into jewellery. It consists of heating and gradually cooling the metal, which softens it, removes its brittleness to make it malleable for working into shapes or hammering flat into sheets.

Hammering [*tarq*] is the term applied to the techniques of hammering annealed metal into flat sheets of uniform thickness in readiness for cutting into the required shapes for bending and/or soldering. In the case of ornaments in the round, embossing is the next stage, followed by repoussé, repoussé chasing, soldering, chasing, and engraving.

These light-weight *asawir*, have been made by hammering. The bracelets are hinged with pin fastenings but the original pins and "safety" chains are missing. The ornaments were achieved by hammering the annealed silver into thin, flat sheets, cutting to shape, and embossing two halves to roundness prior to soldering them together. The designs were carried out with various punches. By their worn appearance they would appear to be old *asawir*, but there is no way of knowing exactly when they were made. As is the case with many other hollow bracelets, pebbles have been trapped inside.

The finials are polyhedrons. Polyhedral finials were typical of bracelets worn in the Fatimid Period, between the 10th and 12th centuries (909–1171) when jewellery of high quality was produced. The Fatimid treasuries surpassed those of all other Muslim dynasties. It was an Islamic custom to present jewellery as gifts and rewards; and it was exchanged amongst rulers.

The Fatimid rulers of Egypt and Syria were ultimately suppressed by the Muslim warrior hero of Crusader fame, Saladin, 1137–1193, Sultan of Egypt.

EMBOSSING & REPOUSSEÉ

زخرفة وبروز

Embossing [*zakhrafa*] and repousse [*buruz*] are decorative techniques in which the design, or domed pattern or shape, is hammered out from the back of a thin piece of metal. The sheet is first laid on a bed of pitch or a shaped mould and the desired patterns are beaten out with variously shaped punches from the back, achieving the relief decoration on the front.

Some of the most beautiful Bedouin earrings and nose-rings owe their decoration to this method. Often resembling the decorative technique of granulation at a glance, the edges of these popular half-moon shaped ornaments are punched from the back to show a delicate beaded border on the front. This worked sheet of metal is then usually fixed to a plain metal backing. The domed backs of scarab beetle-shaped pendants are also created this way before soldering.

Most objects in the round, such as large beads and hollow bracelets, are made by embossing [*zakhrafa*]. The sheet of annealed metal is worked twice over a mould, the second time can be a mould of reverse shape necessary to create the second half of the object, which is then soldered to form the finished product. An ancient method, it has been popular down through the ages because solid cast objects use too much metal. This is one technique which could be achieved by machinery.

Hollow bracelets similar to the pair shown here are typical of those worn, one on each wrist, by the Bedouin women of the Western Province of Saudi Arabia.

These bracelets are the best examples of the repoussé technique shown in this book. The body of the *asawir* which has been decorated by repoussé is enhanced by an overlaid section holding set stones, one of which is green, raising the question as to whether it was made on the Arabian Peninsula. Green stones are rarely found in Arabia.

Shelagh Weir, a noted authority on the Bedouin cultures of Syria and Jordan, has written that green stones, *kharaz al kabseh*, are believed in those countries to be an effective way of preventing postnatal infections, while white stones for a Syrian or Jordanian Bedouin mother are supposed to promote lactation. Also, in these countries, blue beads, known as *'uwayneh*, and other blue stones are worn as protection against the Evil Eye, believed in many parts of the world to be the malignant powers of the envious. Red stones, it is written, were believed by the ancients to have the power to stop all sorts of bleeding and inflammation. They are still worn in Afghanistan for good health and as protection against eye disease.

Overleaf: Silver beads as big as mandarins make an unusually attractive necklace [*iqd*]. Constructed of two embossed halves, these beads were decorated before and after the two halves were soldered together. Bedouin beads are rarely this size. Although the beads are of fine silver, the large, cylindrical charm case, *hirz*, is not. The additional hardness of lower-grade silver is fortunate as this end-opening receptacle may not have survived in pure silver. Many fine old examples have been holed or flattened for their purity. The applied decoration includes twisted wire and also beaded wire, the latter also decorating the beads.

As the necklace is not large enough to be worn, it must be assumed that some beads are missing, certainly the terminals and possibly the beads and charm case do not appear to belong together.

زخرفة	*zakhrafa*
بروز	*buruz*
أساور	*asawir*
خرز الكبسه	*kharaz al kabseh*
عوينه	*'uwayneh*
عقد	*iqd*
حرز	*hirz*
حجاب	*hijab*

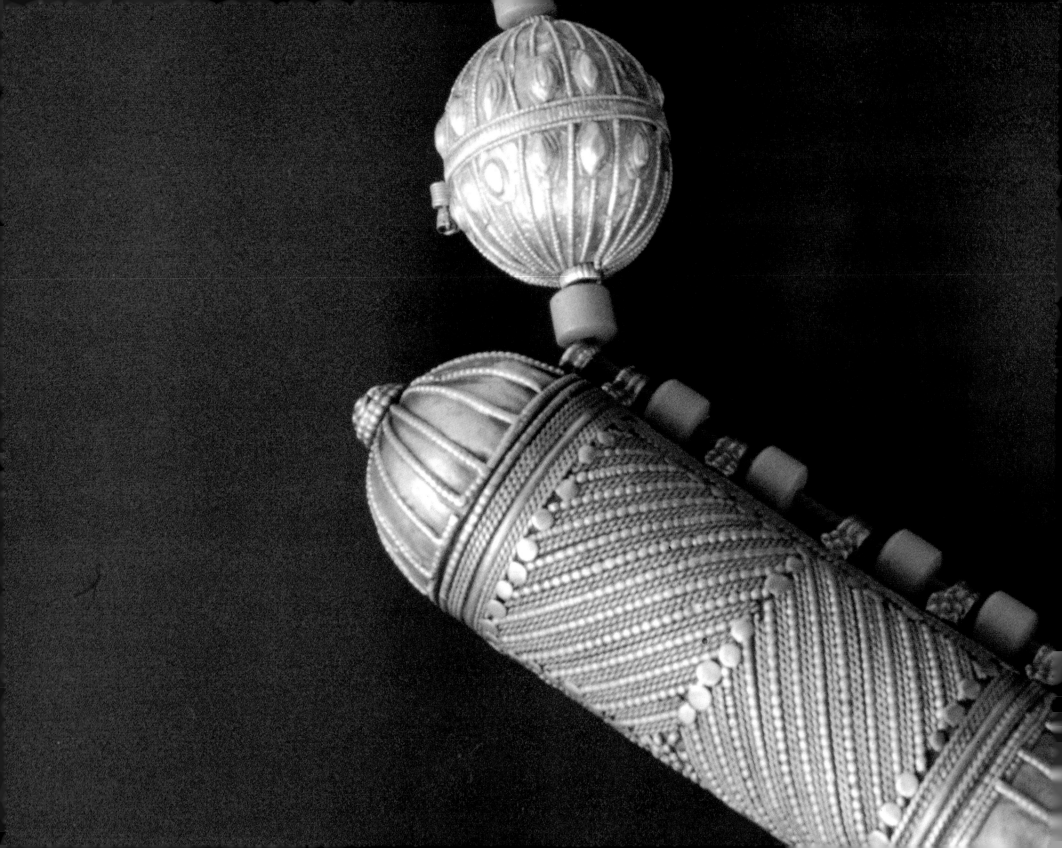

FUSING & SOLDERING

صهر ولِحام

صهر   *sahr*
لِحام   *liham*
مرامي   *marami*
مطاحين   *mata'hin*

Fusing [*sahr*] is the method of amalgamating two metal objects into one whole by melting with intense heat and using copper carbonate. This joining technique is employed to make fine filigreed wire and tiny metal granules and shapes adhere cleanly to a plain surface. Soldering [*liham*], generally called "hard soldering", in relation to jewellery, is the method used for assembling the basic parts of a piece of jewellery. A similar metal is used to join the pieces but one that is alloyed to a lower melting point than the ornament. A flux, the agent to facilitate fusion, is also used to help molten metal flow.

Thin silver rings and the high-bezel silver rings usually display typical granulated decoration, while the shanks of the belled coin rings exhibit applied filigree relief. The dates on some small denominational coins are obliterated but one can often read that they were issued in the time of King Abd al-Aziz bin Abdulrahman al Saud, founder of the Kingdom of Saudi Arabia.

Thin silver rings without bezels, called *marami*, are worn in twos, threes, and fours. They come from the Wadi Dawasir Region. The coined and belled rings, often called *mata'hin*, are from Najran. Some Bedouin women claim that the silver bezelled thin rings were mostly worn by men. The silver rings shown here include two Saudi Arabian coins trimmed with a fringe of tiny balls, an Indian Rupee, a cabochon-cut green stone bezel, a silver-pinned brown stone, and the "*shahid*", a flat-bezelled ring with a point which is worn towards the finger-nail on the forefinger. This example is set with a small red stone and there are tiny pendant balls. A Muslim can point this ring towards Mecca when uttering the Islamic doctrinal formula: "There is no god but God, and Mohammed is his Prophet." It is said that rings of this shape were worn as toe-rings in the south of the Arabian Peninsula.

CHASING & ENGRAVING

نقش وحفر

Chasing [*naqsh*] is a decorative technique in which the design is struck on metal by blows from a punch from the front of the ornament. It is a technique which resembles embossing and repoussé, except that it is performed on the other side of the metal.

There are two types of chasing: flat and repousse. Flat chasing decorates the front of a piece of smooth metal without cutting away any of it. Repoussé chasing is applied to the front surface in the same manner, but it brings out the detail of a raised pattern which has previously been beaten or embossed from the back. Decorative punches can also be used with this technique to achieve a repeated pattern. Skilful chasing is often used in conjunction with engraving to achieve extremely beautiful floral motifs and geometric designs.

Engraving [*hafr*] is quite different from the other decorative techniques. It is often used immediately after hammering, prior to shaping and soldering. Engraving is done by working the surface of the metal with a sharp pointed tool called a graver, which gives a clean and sensitive line often necessary for delicate, linear floral patterns. Fine engraving gives an exquisite high-light to good silver, but effective designs can also be achieved with the graver by the simple scoring of the surface with geometric designs or the gouging out of a repeated simple motif. Often religious amulets are inscribed with the name of Allah by the technique of engraving.

Of good weight and finely worked in excellent silver, this rectangular charm case, with its interesting pendants and intricate chain, makes a handsome necklace. Two methods of embellishment have been employed on the body of the ornament: repoussé chasing and flat chasing. Filigree has been used to outline the pendant charms, *hijab*. These may be a stylized version of the "Hand of Fatima", an amuletic shape often seen as a pendant to Bedouin jewellery. The origin of this charm has been attributed to the virtuous daughter of the Prophet Mohammed. Perhaps these charms are merely "opening pistachios".

نقش *naqsh*
حفر *hafr*

GRANULATION

حبيّة *habbiyat*

Granulation [*habbiyat*], is the art of applying minute metal grains in patterns to a metal surface to produce a raised, three-dimensional decorative effect. It is one of the most difficult and painstaking ornamental techniques, requiring the minute pieces of metal to be fused to a metal surface, rather than soldered, to make a cleaner join.

Surfaces richly decorated with granulation similar to Arabian Bedouin jewellery are characteristic of the Egyptian ornaments taken from the tombs of the Pharaohs. This technique was also employed by the ancient Greeks. The Etruscans became the greatest experts in granulation and their method of application has never been satisfactorily imitated. When their culture was gradually absorbed by the Romans, the art of granulation was largely replaced by that of filigree. Jewellers today do not cease to marvel at the exquisite workmanship of the Etruscan craftsmen.

Granulation, which began crudely in the third millenium BC, reached technical perfection by the eighth and seventh centuries BC. This subsequently lost skill remained a puzzle until an English metallurgist, H.A.P. Litterdale, devised the technique of colloidal hard soldering. This produced results close to those achieved by the ancients. Litterdale omitted the use of convensional flux in favour of a copper hydroxide paste, upon which the tiny granules were arranged. When heated, this medium decomposed into copper oxide and then into copper, to form an invisible join between the granule and the surface being decorated.

The Etruscans used spheres $\frac{1}{10}$ th mm in size – very much smaller than those seen on rustic Bedouin jewellery.

Two relief techniques are visible here – lavish granulation using silver grains and diamond shapes, and liberal plaited filigree and both techniques have been applied elaborately for exotic effect.

These distinctly Oriental-looking bracelets are praiseworthy examples of the rich use of relief ornamentation. Their lustre and silky patina indicate a high silver content. Similar ornaments often appear in larger sizes as anklets.

The domed finials on these old bracelets are set at the end of the tapering tube that has been made from sheet silver. The front face is overlaid by a flat diamond-shaped plaque which has applied embellishment, worn smooth by time.

WIRE & WROUGHT METAL

سلك ومعدن مطرَّز

سلك   *silk*

مدان مطرّز   *madan mutarraz*

أساور   *asawir*

حجل (جمع حجول)   *hijl (pl. hujul)*

Wire [*silk*], as a decorative element in jewellery, has a long history. Early craftsmen hammered thin strips of flat metal to roundness or rolled it to round form between bronze plates. Sometimes, thick wire was fashioned by casting. Hollow wire was made by twisting gold strips around a mandrel which was afterwards withdrawn. But it was difficult to make wire of an even gauge by these methods. Twisted wire in jewellery was popular with the Greeks and later the Romans, who eventually evolved the drawplate as a method by which wire could be tugged through successively smaller holes until it was reduced to the required even gauge.

Byzantium developed the use of wire for ornamentation and carried it forward into the Age of Islam.

Bedouin jewellery reveals a liberal use of wire, often plaited, or woven in loose or tight weave, or sometimes merely twisted. It is invariably used to accent shape. The wire made by the Bedouin craftsmen is also required for their fine filigree and various styles of chain.

Wrought metal [*madan mutarraz*] is metal which is worked into shape by twisting or bending after being made malleable by annealing. The heavy Bedouin pieces, opposite, are wrought and the finest use of this technique can be seen in this twisted "Celtic" style of Central Arabian ornament.

Here, on the torque necklace and in three different sizes of the same *asawir* style the largest being uncomfortably heavy and weighing approximately two hundred grammes – twisted wire appears in relief on wrought metal [*madan mutarraz*]. This torque and bracelets, startlingly similar to first century BC Celtic, are silver rods twisted in tight weave, finished off with cast-on finials, and ornamented [in the case of the smaller-ones] with filigree and granulation. This Celtic style is commonly found in Central Arabia, where it is known as *hijl* in the singular and *hujul* in the plural. The central pair of bracelets illustrates the softness of fine silver. This picture also conveys the lustre of good quality silver. It is unfortunate that the filigree twisted wire has worn away from the grooves and that the roundness of the wrought rods is lost. Some examples of this style, fashioned in low-grade silver, are in perfect condition but they have a core of copper, visible occasionally when a finial has been snapped off.

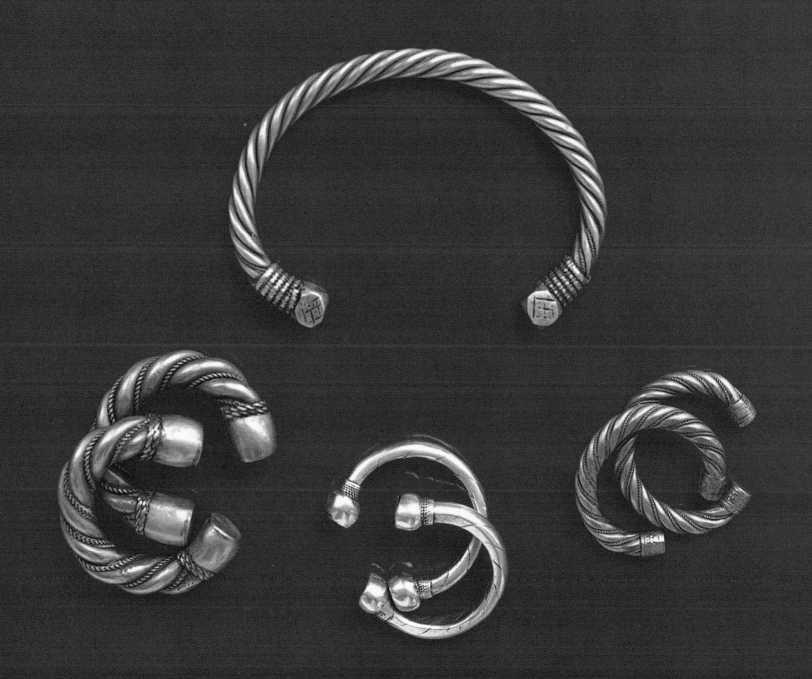

CHAIN-MAKING

صناعة السلاسل

Chain-making [*amal silsilah*] is yet another technique for working silver. Hand-made chain [*silsilah*] is a principal element of Bedouin jewellery – often the major part of the ornament. Bedouin chained ornaments are constructed with many different types of links, spacers and baubles, sometimes combining the techniques of filigree, granulation and sand-casting. The plainer, more crudely executed types of chain seem to be the natural progression from the earliest use of wire in jewellery: a series of simple connections to link baubles together without decorative pretension.

Low-grade silver is invariably used for chains, presumably because silver is stronger when alloyed with more base metal.

The *jnad* is an enormous piece of surprisingly lightweight jewellery worn under one arm, usually the left. Its giant bells jangle gaily when they are moved. The large pendants are attached to a herring-bone-patterned rope, an intricate piece of work created with silver wire. Several decorative jewellery-making techniques are exhibited on this ornament, notably applied work such as filigree and a coarse form of granulation on the charm cases. The crescent-shaped pendants have been decorated with repoussé chasing in addition.

The crescents, twin oval-bodied rectangular charm cases, and triangular charm case, all support pendant bells and balls which have been embossed and decorated with beaded wire, appearing also on the other elements of this ornament.

عمل سلسلة   *amal silsilah*
سلسلة   *silsilah*
علاقة   *'ilaqah*

FILIGREE

مُشبَّك

مشبك	*mushabbak*
علاقة	*'ilaqah*
حلق أو خرص	*halaq or khurs*

Filigree [*mushabbak*] is a decorative technique which can be executed in two ways: "*à jour*" or "applied". *A jour* – "open" like lace – is a high ornamental technique achieved by twisting and forming wire into delicate tracery to make various patterns which are then soldered for solidity. With the applied method, the twisted wire patterns are cleanly fused to the ornament by intense heat rather than soldered. Variations include patterned and tightly twisted lengths of wire placed to accentuate shape. The applied method of filigree is the more commonly employed.

The ancient Greeks were expert with filigree and favoured such delicate and detailed decoration for jewellery embellishment in preference to gems. A great deal of Arabian Bedouin jewellery reflects this preference.

Left: These fine examples of Bedouin silver jewellery are quite old and exhibit signs of wear, but they are fortunately intact, having been constructed of relatively poor silver.

Circular 'medallion' pendants come from all regions of Arabia. The examples shown here are from North Yemen where there is a tradition for fine filigree. The size, weight and embellishment varies yet the patterns always outline and/or confirm the shape and never cross the medallion. The body of the example (front) is constructed of filigree overlaid with circles of tiny applied filigree rosette motifs surmounted by little spheres divided by beaded wire – the whole circled by pairs of wire coils meeting to form a serrated edge. As shown, pendants suspended from the edges of the bottom halves of these medallions, vary in style.

CASTING

سكيب

Sand-casting [*sakb*] is not as popular as the other jewellery manufacturing methods because it uses more metal; yet casting results in a three-dimensional object and is a method of reproducing a piece accurately, rapidly and inexpensively so far as labour cost is involved.

To produce a cast object, the jewellers of the ancient world and the creators of Bedouin jewellery today first make a mould by pressing the model between a pair of iron frames which are packed tightly with very fine sand. The mould is then divided and the model removed, after which the sand is treated with a mixture of alum, salt and sugar in water to preserve the impression. The mould is reassembled and molten metal poured through an opening previously prepared for the purpose. The cast copy is then removed and the mould discarded as it can be used only once.

This pair of heavy and cumbersome bracelets or armlets may originally have been a style worn by men. In any event, they are still in demand and the silversmiths of Arabia continue to make them solely for indigenous folk as this style does not appeal to Western visitors.

It is likely that they were cast wholly or partially in the past and each pair varies in method of construction today. The protuding nodules resemble giant granulation and it can be seen here that the balls finally placed overlay filigree wound around the body of the bracelet. The affixed central medallions have applied decoration.

سكب *sakb*

GEMSTONE CUTTING

قطع جوهرة

A lapidary's art includes the cutting, polishing and generally shaping of gemstones for ornamental use. Although quite different from a gemologist, a lapidary depends on the science of gemology, requiring to know a gemstone's true identity and characteristics to know how it is going to behave.

The art of stone cutting originated among the ancient Babylonians and Egyptians, gradually advancing until it reached excellence in ancient Greece and Rome. Cut gems are used in Arabian Bedouin jewellery but stone cutting is not usually carried out on the Peninsula. Generally, the stones set in Bedouin jewellery are not "cut", but merely shaped. Garnets present an exception and often appear fashioned in different ways, either cabochon, faceted or engraved. The cabochon and faceted cuts are the most important methods for fashioning gems and the more commonly seen of the three techniques used for red stones in Bedouin jewellery.

The word "cabochon" comes from the Old French *cabo*, meaning head, and refers to the rounded top of the stone, a style developed mainly to prepare gemstones to fit standard mountings. There are three forms for the cabochon: the highest dome called "double cabochon"; the usual, medium dome called "high cabochon"; and the shallow dome called "tallow-topped". This cabochon shape was very popular for Roman rings, and remains today the most popular cut for garnets set in Arabian Bedouin jewellery. Turquoise commonly appears around the world cut as a cabochon but is rarely seen so in Bedouin ornaments.

To facet a gem, for many in the lapidary craft, is the ultimate achievement. Faceting, like all gemstone cutting [*qat' jauharah*], consists of grinding and polishing gemstones with successively finer grades of abrasives, and it takes great skill to do it well. Lapidaries have been faceting gemstones with methods that have changed little over hundreds of years; the finest and most valuable gems are almost always cut in this way because the faceted planes make the maximum use of the optical properties of the gemstone.

Engraved red stones are occasionally seen in traditional Bedouin jewellery and the designs were perhaps once symbolic. More often, a large red stone is inscribed "Allah". The garnet [*aqiq ahmar*], being hard and durable, is a worthy subject for the great skill of the engraver.

Intaglio is the name given to an engraved stone where the design has been sunk into the surface, in the opposite fashion to cameo cutting where the background of the subject is cut away. The Greeks were the finest exponents of intaglio in the ancient world: it is recorded that they began their engraving of hard stones in the fourth century BC. The Greeks passed their skill on to the Romans and intaglio became a greater art form as efforts were made to ensure the subject suited the colour of stone upon which it was executed.

The garnets in these three single asawir *are fashioned by different methods: cabochon, faceted and engraved*

قطع جوهره   *qat'jauharah*

عقيق أحمر   *aqiq ahmar*

أساور   *asawir*

5 MATERIALS

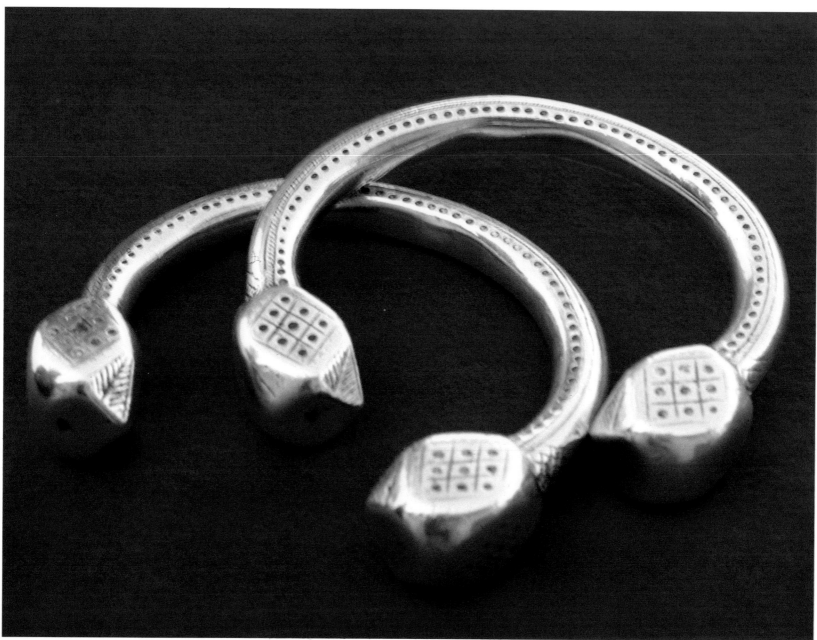

SILVER

فضة

UNLIKE GOLD, silver is not found in its pure state; it must be separated from the other constituents of the ore. The natural alloy of the precious metals, silver and gold, known as electrum, was thought by the ancient Greeks to be another metal, and silver as a separate element was discovered accidentally as a by-product of the gold-refining process.

Silver [*fiddah*] is less malleable than gold and also less stable, corroding quite readily and tarnishing when exposed to sulphur compounds in the air. Although as much silver jewellery as gold may have been made in the ancient world, this is hard to prove, because all but a few silver pieces have perished. People who possess silver, whether it be superb "sterling" or excellent to inexpensive "plated", are generally quite ignorant about it. This is lamentable if only because some knowledge of silver is vital to its proper care and preservation. Silver should be kept from the air as much as possible and tarnish removed regularly. Standard silver has 925 parts of pure silver with 75 parts of alloyed base metal to the 1,000 total. This ratio varies greatly in Bedouin silver ornaments.

The most common question concerning Bedouin jewellery is whether the silver is "real" or not. Most Bedouin traditional jewellery does not contain silver, but the silver content varies from piece to piece. Silver objects are rarely made of pure silver but usually an alloy. As silver is soft, the craftsman adds a base metal to make the object durable; he usually uses copper, which gives the best sheen. "Sterling" silver is made to a strict formula laid down by experts and objects stamped "sterling" should be of high silver content, *ie* 92.5 per cent, rendered adequately durable by the copper additive. The finest pieces of "sterling" silver are hallmarked by an Assay Office as a guarantee of quality and adherence to the prescribed formula. Bedouin jewellery is never hallmarked, but sometimes carries the mark of the silversmith. Plated silver is too large a subject for inclusion here, and it does not relate to the silver jewellery worn by the Bedouin.

All of the pieces of Bedouin silver jewellery are made of an alloy. A collector will become accustomed to recognizing higher or lower silver content in Bedouin jewellery by handling the items and becoming familiar with them. The higher the silver content, the richer the sheen and the more velvety the touch. Shallow incised or punched designs are quite often worn away because of the softness of the high-grade silver, but the smooth and silky patina which remains is very beautiful and easy to recognize. The more lead-like the appearance of the ornament, the less is the silver therein. Copper, tin and zinc are the base metals added to make the alloys used in Bedouin jewellery manufacture.

Despite the custom of melting down Bedouin jewellery on the death of its owner, the new ornaments which are then re-created with the metal may be identical to the original because traditional designs and styles are preferred; but it is possible that with each successive melting, more base metal is added; and the workmanship may be better or worse than previously. A collector of Bedouin silver jewellery seeks the optimum combination: the best examples of traditional pieces; the highest silver content, and the most accomplished workmanship. One should also observe the weight of an object. Two items may look identical in every way, but one may contain more metal and therefore be heavier, which makes it a more valuable addition to a collection.

Before being fashioned into jewellery, silver must first be worked up into sheets or wire, unless it is to be used for casting. Like many other metals, both silver and gold become harder as they are worked. Brittleness may occur unless the annealing process – heating to redness and cooling at regular intervals – is used to relieve the stresses.

Some Bedouin buttons are made from sheets of beaten gold folded over a packing agent, such as wood, but non-cast silver ornaments in the round are always hollow, constructed from sheet metal. The silver ornaments are generally fashioned from thicker sheets of metal, which do not need packing to resist damage; yet, many lovely pieces of fine old silver Bedouin

Created from fine silver, these attractive horseshoe-shaped bracelets gleam without cleaning. They are very simply decorated by scoring the surface and using a punch. The original design has worn away considerably because of the softness of this high-grade silver, but a smooth and silky patina is the result of the years of wear. The punch work is actually chasing (naqsh) while the scoring is defined as engraving (hafr).

jewellery become damaged, because the metal employed was too thin or the object has been made of almost pure silver, with an inadequate amount of base metal to withstand wear and tear.

Tiny geometrical shapes, especially triangles, diamonds and circles, are cut out of sheet silver which has been beaten very thin and these provide relief decoration on Arabian Bedouin jewellery. These minute shapes are affixed to larger thicker beaten silver shapes, also mostly geometrical, and various other ornaments. The moon shapes, full, half and crescent are popular, the crescent usually worn inverted.

The shape of the ornament is usually accented with filigreed silver wire and granulated silver spheres, often called shot. When circles are used, they are generally embellished with pendants on the inside edge as well as the outside edge.

Silver beads are commonly incorporated into Bedouin necklaces and appear as the largest beads on the strand, placed at regular intervals for relief. The terminal mace-shaped bead on an Arabian necklace is also usually made from silver, fashioned from a piece of metal folded over, a more economical method of production than drilling solid silver. Many small silver beads are constructed this way but large silver Bedouin beads, sometimes up to two inches in diameter, are constructed in two halves by the technique of embossing; they range from annular, bulbous, cylindrical to spherical. Two mace-shaped beads identical to those fashioned by today's Arabian Bedouin

jeweller, albeit fashioned in gold were found in the Jawan tomb excavations in the Eastern Province of Arabia, dated about 100 AD, and were common to Greek jewellery of the fourth century BC.

Another question commonly raised about Bedouin jewellery is the source of the silver. One explanation is that Maria Theresa thalers and Turkish silver majeedis were melted down and fashioned into ornaments. However it is obvious by the amount of jewellery available that this cannot have been the only source; in all likelihood silver was imported from a number of areas, entering the Peninsula by the various ports. This speculation is strengthened by the fact that Arabian mines have only recently been reopened after hundreds of years of inactivity. Yet, with the knowledge that Bedouin silver ornaments have been recreated perhaps many times, some of the silver may come from ancient yields.

The study of coins has led to the development of a method which could determine accurately the source of Bedouin jewellery silver, at least in the case of the oldest examples.

Until lately it was necessary to damage coins to analyse their metal content, but by the method developed at the University of Michigan, only a tiny rubbing is taken from the edge of the coin on a piece of roughed high-purity quartz. This quartz can be irradiated with neutrons from a nuclear reactor and the metal made radioactive. From the types and amounts of radioactivity found on the quartz, it is then possible to determine the fineness of the coin that was sampled, and

discover the amounts of impurities, such as the level of gold impurity in a silver coin.

Ancient and medieval metallurgists apparently did not realize that many silver sources contain as much as one per cent gold as an impurity, and therefore did not attempt to remove this precious constituent. This is fortunate, since the level of impurities in old silver coins can provide us with valuable historical information. Each ancient silver source had its own characteristic level of gold impurity and this level was unaltered by the crude silver-refining processes used by the metallurgists. For example, two silver coins may appear the same but analysis of their metal content will give an indication of the origin of the mother lode. This basic method could be applied to the oldest examples of Arabian Bedouin jewellery and perhaps allow us to determine the actual source of silver used for these ornaments.

Note: As a wedding anniversary symbol, silver represents twenty-five years.

This ornament, hilyat sha'r, *from Central Arabia is worn draped over the back of the* head, *attached to a head-band by means of hooks soldered to the back of the side plaques which exhibit applied decoration.*

فضّة   *fiddah*

حلية شعر   *hilyat sha'r*

90

GOLD & BRASS

Gold is the metal-worker's ideal medium, for it is the most malleable, ductile and durable of materials: a goldsmith may draw it into wire as fine as a hair or beat it into leaf, so thin that the light will shine through it. It may be cast with a finger print or smelted into minute spheres known as 'shot'.

The proportion of gold in an alloy is measured in carats, pure gold being assessed at twenty-four carats. Gold is obtained in two ways – either in nugget form in river beds from alluvial sources or by mining. It is supposed that gold was first discovered in the sixth millennium BC from alluvial deposits. It is found all over the world and every race, with the exception of the New Zealand Maori, has shown interest in it. The chief sources today are South Africa, Australia and Russia.

Pure gold is remarkably stable and impervious to the ordinary processes of corrosion and decay: a gold coin can lie buried for more than a thousand years and yet be found as if newly minted. Appreciated for its beauty and rarity by the ancients, it is on account of its inherent stability that it is possible to study the jewellery-making techniques evolved by past civilizations.

Opposite: The head-dress jewel [ilaqsh] has one faceted red stone surrounded by turquoise; the pendants resemble silver pistachios. The body of the ornament is overlaid with sheet gold. To the rlght, eight of these Bedouin buttons [azrsr] – singualar, zirr] are made from sheet gold over packing, while some are hollow silver.

Bedouin jewellery, although predominantly silver, traditionally includes some gold ornaments, but the techniques involved are generally limited to hammering to make flat sheets for cutting and granulation for the surface decoration.

As late as the nineteenth century, gold and silver, because of the beliefs surrounding them, contributed to the breaking-up of an empire. The Ashanti people, who occupy the south-central area of the country known, until 1957, as the Gold Coast when it was re-named Ghana, had – besides a reputation for being one of the most war-like tribes in West Africa – an extremely high standard of gold workmanship. Their remaining beaten gold ornaments attest to exceptional skill.

Since the foundation of the Ashanti Confederacy in the latter part of the seventeenth century, the Commander of the right wing of their army traditionally sat upon a stool wrought from silver. The Asantehene [ruler] occupied a golden stool, which, according to Ashanti tradition, was created by the magic of a priest for the legendary figure Osei Tutu, the actual founder of the Confederation. The stool was believed to contain the soul of the Ashanti nation, and taboos surrounded it together with religious and superstitious beliefs.

According to William Tordoff, at the inception of the Confederacy, the Ashanti established contact with the European trading companies on the Guinea Coast, and their successive kings founded a nation which grew powerful. Latterly, during a period of internal disorder in the reign of King Prempeh (1888–1935), the British, in their administrative capacity, whilst professing friendship to the King and his people, became preoccupied with self-interest, desiring to establish a trade monopoly on the Nile.

The King, as occupant of the Golden Stool, was guardian of the ancestral spirits of the Ashanti and thus the cornerstone of the constitution. Through him the people might have been reconciled. Instead, the British denied help in uniting Prempeh's strife-torn people, compounding this disaster by failing to comprehend the power of the gold throne. Yet, the British recognized the Golden Stool as a useful political tool and in so using it, went on to commit further tactless acts and errors of political judgement which resulted in the desecration of the revered seat and the complete disintegration of the Ashanti Empire.

Note: As a wedding anniversary symbol, gold represents fifty years.
Arabian Gold: See Middle Eastern Mining pg 115.

Brass

Brass too, is used for some Bedouin ornaments, but generally it seems to be as a yellow metal substitute for gold, as it was customary for the jeweller to cater for the needs of the poorer Bedouin as well as the richer. This is borne out by the fact that the traditional oval forehead ornaments, displaying set turquoise with garnets and pendant pearls, are occasionally seen in brass.

أزرار (مفرد زر) *azrar (sing. zirr)*

TURQUOISE

فيروز

The name "turquoise" originated from the fact that the Persian stones from Khorasan were exported through Turkey: the French called it "Turkish stone" or "pierre turquoise". The ancient names for turquoise were "callais" and "callaite".

Tales have been attached to gemstones through the ages and turquoise is no exception. It is said that it will glow when the wearer is content but, when sad, the sheen disappears. Turquoise is never transparent and usually coarse; it is never faceted and mostly cut as cabochon, although Arabian Bedouin jewellery, with rare exception, does not display it this way. It is invariably merely shaped and used in flat form, rough-polished, raised to prominence by the setting.

To keep the original colour and sheen, turquoise should not come into contact with grease, oil, strong chemicals, excessive heat or unnecessary abrasion, for any such marring is irreversible. However it is claimed that the palest colour may be improved by dipping into blue wax.

Towards the end of the fourth millennium BC the Egyptians were already mining turquoise in the Sinai Peninsula near Serabit-el-Khadem. Turquoise scarabs were found in the tombs of the Pharaohs, and turquoise was much favoured by the Chinese and the Aztecs, both for adornment and religious purposes. There were major sources in Persia, China and North America. The streaked form used by the Bedouin jewellers, called Turquoise Matrix, is found in Western Arabia, as well as in north and south Yemen. Matrix is the stone in which gemstone is found.

[Rey Urban, the celebrated Swedish silversmith whose work reflects the ultra-modern Scandinavian jewellery trends, has noted that matrix turquoise is preferred by his clientele].

The finest turquoise comes today from the Nishapur district in Iran, as it has done for many thousands of years. So perfect are these stones that it is difficult to tell them from fakes. No stone has been imitated with greater success – in glass, porcelain and by chemical composition. And, nowadays, turquoise dust can be moulded together with synthetic resin too, to achieve an excellent imitation.

Note: As a birthstone, turquoise represents the month of December.

The central five hair ornaments [*hilyat sha'r*] [*opposite*] have silver mounts and are a rare find as they are usually brass, like the outer two. The middle piece has a gold pin which is also unusual, although central pins of this kind are occasionally seen as Bedouin finger-rings. All mounts have embossed and applied filigree edges. These ornaments are sometimes worn appliqué, sewn to clothing, but for the hair, tresses are traditionally threaded through the loops of seven pieces at the back of the head.

The gemstones are turquoise [*fairuz*].

حلية شعر *hilyat sh'ar*
فيروز *fairuz*

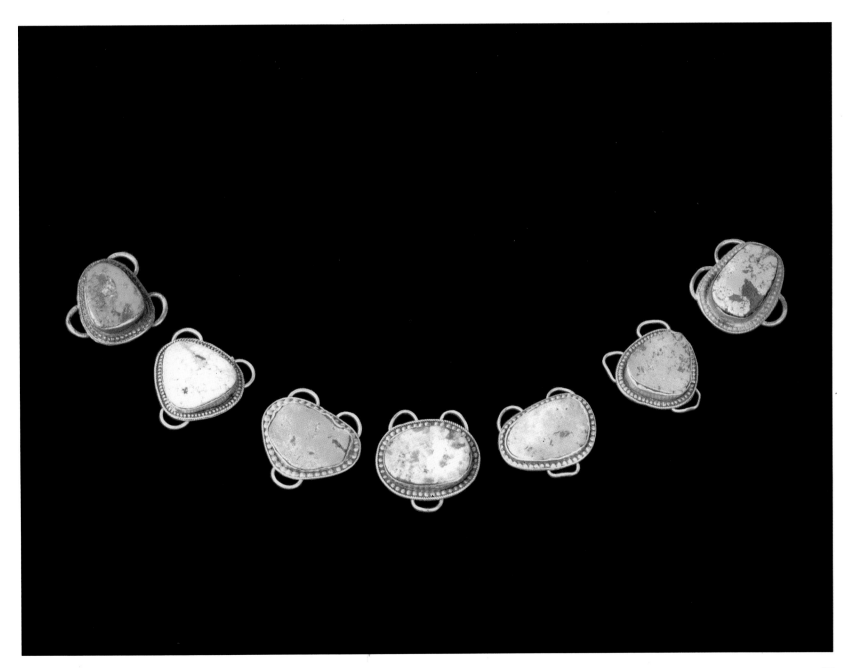

GARNET

عقيق أحمر

Commonly a rich ruby red, garnets are characteristic of Arabian Bedouin jewellery, generally used in conjunction with turquoise.

The word "garnet" is said to have come from the Latin "granum" meaning grain, since garnets frequently occur like grains in the surrounding rock. Another theory claims that the name is derived from the inner colour of the pomegranate. The Bedouin called them *aqiq ahmar*, a name which they share with the carnelian. It means "semi-precious stone". Garnets occur in very ancient jewellery. It was with the Romans that garnet rose to a new prominence as a jewel. They were particularly popular, too, in a relatively recent period, the Victorian Age. Some fine garnet-encrusted jewellery is presently seen around the world, made in Czechoslovakia; but the stones are small, the smallest being the fine deep ruby colour such as is widely found in Victorian jewellery.

Garnets are not always red. They are beautiful stones of high lustre and strong colour and are fairly hard and durable. They are relatively abundant, with several different sub-species, one of which, the green demantoid garnet, is a most valuable stone. Various types of garnet occur in numerous places, perhaps the best known being a large area near Trebenice, in the Bohemian region of Czechoslovakia. There is also a brownish-red variety which comes from the gravel beds of Ceylon and the Arabian Peninsula.

Note: As a birthstone, garnet represents January, and under the signs of the Zodiac, it belongs to Aquarius.

Such excellent workmanship as this is rare. The decoration for these tubular, hinged and pinned *asawir* was carried out with a decorative punch using the technique of chasing. The stones have been set in secure but simple settings with fluted trimming. Two cabochon garnets contrast with rough-polished, flat turquoise. The combination of red and blue stones is traditional, although the stones are not always turquoise and garnet. The fact that red stones, whether carnelian, garnet or glass, are used interchangeably by the Bedouin jewellers, stresses the traditional importance of a red stone whatever the value.

The hinge pins have been replaced with copper and the clasp pins and chains are missing.

عقيق أحمر *aqiq ahmar*
أساور *asawir*

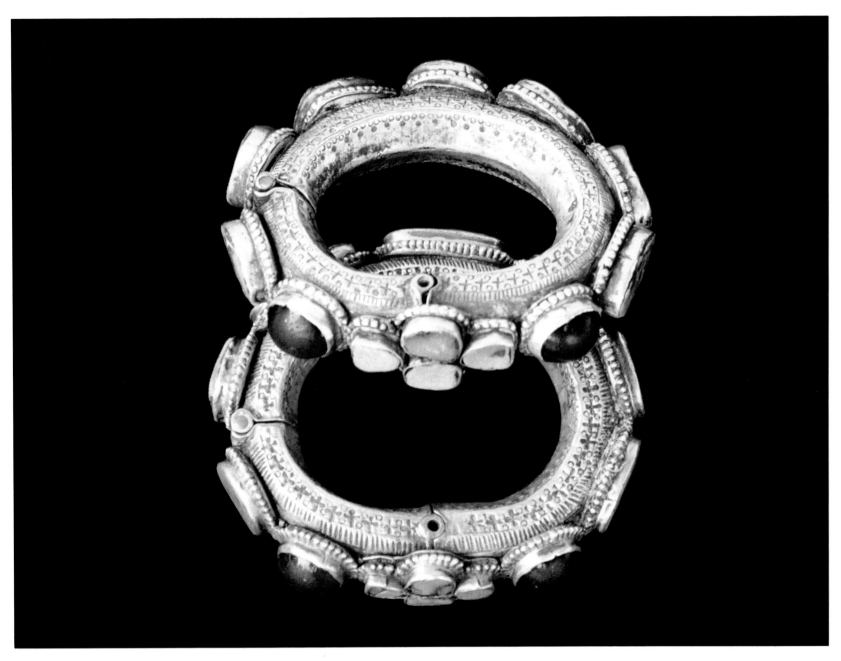

CARNELIAN

عقيق أحمر

Carnelian, the brownish-red semi-transparent stone which is used in Bedouin jewellery interchangeably with garnet and red glass has also been appreciated for thousands of years. Carnelian [*aqiq ahmar*] is a quartz and most of the stones used in jewellery fall into this category. It is often a glowing orange-red colour, which can be imitiated in glass. However, glass imitations always have bubbles present. Carnelian, like turquoise, was mined on the Sinai Peninsula by the ancients. Many of the beads, some hand-painted, which are found on the Peninsular sites of ancient civilizations, are carnelian.

Often called cornelian, it was a favoured stone of the Roman engravers who made imaginative intaglios combining subject matter involving the colour of the gem. Cows grazed on green jasper, marine deities appeared on aquamarine, and the flaying of Marsyas was executed in carnelian.

Carnelian and its imitations are popularly used in *mesbaha*, or *subha*, the prayer-bead strands, often referred to in the West as "worry-beads'. *Mesbaha* are carried by the menfolk throughout Arabia.

Prayer-beads have an obscure origin, and it is not clear how they became such an integral part of Arabian appearance. There is nothing in the Koran about them. The custom of carrying a string of beads for the purposes of prayer, is believed to have originated in northern India or Persia; the fashion spreading from there after Alexander the Great conquered the Persians and formed the vast Hellenic Empire. This would account for the existence of similar "worry-beads" appearing throughout Mediterranean countries.

As a rule, there are thirty-three beads in *mesbaha*. These are sectioned in three groups of eleven beads by two spacer beads and one terminal bead which ends with a tassel. Sometimes, there are thirty-three beads between each spacer, making a ninety-nine bead *mesbaha*, claimed by some to represent the ninety-nine attributes of Allah – and claimed by others to represent the ninety-nine appellations for Allah.

A devout Muslim methodically fingers each bead at prayer time, one at a time, intoning Koranic and extemporaneous phrases in praise of Allah, or asking his forgiveness. He may say something different at each bead or repeat the same thing thirty-three times – or eleven times – as it is a custom to change the adoration when a spacer is reached.

Mesbaha are made from every gemstone and precious metals, and the great skills of the finest jewellers now produce exquisite strands. India and Pakistan export scented *kalambaz*, or sandalwood *mesbaha*. In Mecca, there is a wide variety available from plastic and glass to translucent red amber, and Arabia's famed black coral, *yusr*, inlaid with silver. Many pilgrims select a strand as a gift for a friend at home.

Hardy, low-grade silver has prolonged the life of this piece of jewellery. The ornament [*lazm*] demonstrates several methods used in decorating Arabian Bedouin jewellery. Its embellishment with applied floral motifs is unusual: generally, floral motifs are achieved by engraving. This is a rare piece today. It is worn following the line of the chin, to hang before the neck like a screen. The *lazm* is attached near the earlobes to the headgear. Altogether, this is an extremely lovely piece of jewellery.

The stones are carnelian on each side, and faceted garnet in the middle, set in high collets, as are the fake coral beads. Crudely-fashioned charms, which may represent the "Hand of Fatima" are also pendant. The condition of the stones and the ornament suggest it is very old.

Note: Carnelian represents Virgo under the signs of the Zodiac, and is an alternative to ruby as a birthstone for July.

عقيق أحمر *aqiq ahmar*
لزم *lazm*

AMBER

كهرمان

Forty million years ago, soft gluey resin oozed from trees; it hardened, dropped to the ground and was buried until discovered by early man. The ancients were obviously captivated by the beauty of this material which we know as amber, for achaeologists claim that it was treasured in the Stone Age and worn as jewellery for thousands of years.

Amber [*kahraman*] can be clear or opaque, and appears in the latter form as Bedouin beads. It is a comparatively soft material, and burns with a bright flame. Amber was used by Danish tribesmen 15,000 years ago. They carved it into beads from which they formed long necklaces; and hoards of their amber ornaments were buried with their dead in the hope that it would appease the spirits.

Large amounts of this esteemed commodity were a regular part of early trade route treasure, and often cost as much as gold. It was used not only ornamentally but also as a gemological remedy both internally and externally. It was prized by the ancient Greeks not least for its magnetic properties when rubbed: it is from the Greek word for amber *elektron*, that "electric" was coined. Baltic amber was called "Gold of the North" by the Romans – the Baltic cache remained a northern secret until Phoenicians visited the area in about 1,000 BC. The most highly prized amber came for centuries from what is now the Russian Baltic coast source, although it does occur elsewhere. Roman physicians prescribed ointment made from ground amber as a salve for wounds. It was the Roman author Pliny in 77 AD, who first described amber as a

product of the plant world – though legend had asserted amber to be the solidified urine of the lynx [dark for the male, pale for the female]; or even the petrified tears of God. In the Middle Ages, amber reached a peak of popularity and cost as much as gold and silver.

As a fossil resin of pine trees which flourished in the Tertiary Period, amber is a mineral organic compound. It takes its name from the Arabic *anbar* meaning a "combustible material".

Its authenticity can be tested by setting it alight. Real amber floats in very salty water whilst imitations sink, a decidedly more satisfactory test. Amber is found anywhere in the world that such resin-producing trees grew. It is a paradoxical substance, light enough to float in salt water, tough enough to withstand the ravages of time and yet soft enough to be shaped by the most simple tools.

Amber exists in many shades, from black to blue to light-golden brown. Quite often insects are trapped inside, perfectly preserved after millions of years, assisting scientists to learn about the flora and fauna of ancient forests. In the nineteenth century entomologists and botanists, inspired by Darwin's newly formulated theory of evolution, began to study these ancient captives in amber. Unlike other fossil materials, amber is not actually petrified. It remains the identical organic material it was when it flowed from the pines. The pressure of ice and immersion in sea water caused the molecules to rearrange themselves and polymerize changing the resin from a tacky substance to a solid. Geologists call it "succinite".

It is likely that much of the amber used in Bedouin jewellery found its way through Afghanistan. The large cube-shaped amber beads common to Arabian Bedouin ornaments are often seen in Morocco, North Africa, Qatar and Oman. In some countries, amber beads were currency.

The simple tools of the amber-turner's trade have remained virtually unchanged for generations: a wheel, now motorpowered, with discs of stiff cloth mounted on a spindle. The craftsman holds the amber against the spinning cloth and turns it until the raw lump has been rubbed and shaped to the desired form and sheen.

Belled coin pendants and charm cases are commonly found suspended from strands of amber, both real and fake, in colours ranging from clear russet red to opaque and bright yellow. The shapes vary greatly, too, as can be seen from this picture.

كهرمان   *kahraman*
عنبر   *anba*

CORAL

مرجَان

Coral, known as *marjan* in Arabic, is a non-mineral along with jet and pearl: non-minerals represent less than ten per cent of all gemstones. The coral used in Bedouin jewellery is dark pink to red, although precious coral can range from pale pink to red and exists also in white and black.

Coral is "for wisdom": certainly it was sage of early man to include coral with gemstones so many thousands of years ago, for its beauty and rarity. It has been used for centuries as amulets, talismans and for ornamental purposes. The Chinese credited coral with magical properties. The tales surrounding gemstones are indeed fascinating but none more fanciful than the ancient Greeks' legendary explanation of coral being blood which had become hardened after dripping from the severed head of Medusa. In reality large colonies of minute sea animals secrete a continuous hard skeleton of calcium carbonate to make the branch-like structures of coral so treasured by man.

As a gemstone it is easily worked, and became the height of fashion in the nineteenth century. Today the palest pink variety known as "angel skin" is highly prized and used by exclusive Western jewellers.

The finest coral is dredged off the coast of Algeria and Tunisia, and at several points off the coasts of Italy, France and Spain. The coral used in Bedouin jewellery may be imported. It is found in the Red Sea, where the gathering of coral was once a thriving maritime industry. Black coral, 'yusr', from the Red Sea was used to make prayer bead strands.

The rarest prayer bead strand, *mesbaha*, is made from fine old black coral from the Red Sea, between Jeddah and Gonfode. Precious black coral is a lustrous black and takes a fine polish. Traditionally, the price of *yusr* beads was determined by size, and the Jeddah bead-turners sold them in strands of one hundred. Most of Jeddah's black coral was destined for Malaya. Coral farming is no longer an Arabian industry, so old strands, which are commonly inlaid with silver, are keenly sought by collectors.

Note: As a wedding anniversary symbol coral represents thirty-five years.

The double-stranded necklace [right] is a traditional Central Arabian (Najdi) style and it is believed that the threading is original. Such pieces fetch amazingly high prices today and they are very rare. Genuine coral is a chief characteristic of this type of necklace and beads of turquoise, agate, gold and silver are interspersed. One or more tear-shaped agates are invariably included, as are pressed or stamped gold "sequin" pendants and other fine gold pendants and beads set with turquoise.

مرجان *marjan*
حرز *hirz*

PEARL

لؤلؤ

In the past, the finest pearls in the world came from the Arabian Gulf, so it is not surprising that the best old pieces of gold Bedouin jewellery should incorporate pearls. Turn of the century Arabian jewellery, too, makes much use of the small baroque-type pearls, occasionally forming multi-stranded necklaces with relief beads at regular intervals, which are secured with cord ties. Pearls [*lulu*] have been prized for centuries on the Peninsula. Today, the pearls used in Bedouin jewellery are often the cultured variety from Japan. In either case, the pearls are "baroque", *ie* of irregular shape.

When the first cultured pearls appeared in the 1930s, prices of natural pearls collapsed, never to recover. Trading stopped overnight until some positive test could be devised which would distinguish between the two products of the oyster. Although X-rays may reveal the bead core of the cultured pearl, this is not a reliable guide.

Much of Arabia's pearling manpower went to the oilfields, and today, Gulf pearls are rare and expensive.

The measure used for weighing pearls is the "grain" which equals one quarter of a metric carat, the carat being one-fifth of a metric gramme.

Pearl, like other non-mineral gems, has long been treasured by Man and long classified as precious. Nature fashions a pearl when a grain of sand invades the oyster shell, and irritation stimulates the mantle of the animal to pour out a fluid which encases the foreign material in nacre, leaving it as an excrescence on the lining of the shell. To culture pearls, an incision is made in the mantle under aseptic conditions and a bead of freshwater mussel is inserted with a tiny graft of mantle, which, when the mollusc is returned to the sea, envelops the bead entirely, eventually covering it with nacre.

Myths surround pearls, as they surround most precious stones. One of the tales is recorded as "fact": Cleopatra, attempting to impress Mark Anthony, tossed a priceless pearl into her wine goblet and drank the contents once the pearl had dissolved. Experts say that any wine capable of dissolving a pearl would also have done damage to Cleopatra herself. Perhaps then she swallowed the pearl whole.

Another myth persisting into modern times concerns the care of pearls. It is said that pearls must be worn constantly next to the skin to retain their lustre, and that royal families have requested their ladies-in-waiting to wear costly pearls for them, even to bed. In truth, to retain their beauty, pearls should not be exposed to prolonged heat or excessively dry air; and it is essential that they should be cleaned occasionally to remove damaging skin acids.

The body of this slightly convex-shaped oval *kaffat* or *khamasiyat* for the forehead, worn stitched to an unhemmed red textile back, is a sheet of 24 carat gold [*dhahab*]. The stones are turquoise and faceted garnet, and the pendants are "Gulf" baroque pearls, the term applied to the irregular-shaped pearls from the Arabian Gulf. Blue beads sit amongst the pearls.

The jewellery-making techniques used are hammering for the body of the ornament, and applied granulation and filigree for relief. Two fluted and granulated bosses appear at the top. This ornament often appears set solely with turquoise. It also occurs now and again fashioned identically in brass, a yellow metal substitute. It is a piece of jewellery unique to Saudi Arabia's central province it is not imitated in neighbouring countries.

Such traditional ornaments vary only slightly under the hands of their creators and they conform in that the deep collets in which the flat-form turquoise and garnets are set, display granulated frames. Usually applied filigree accents the body of the ornament. Once again, it can be seen how Arabian Peninsular craftsmen and women, in jewellery and costume, accent shape. Turquoise and blue ceramic beads are usually included in the pearl fringe – the pearls speared with gold wire, linked by filigree, and threaded through filigree tubes surrounding the ornament.

لؤلؤ	*lulu*
كفة	*kaffat*
خماسية	*khamasiyat*
ذهب	*dhahab*

Note: As a birthstone, pearl represents June, as an alternative to moonstone and alexandrite. As a wedding anniversary symbol pearl represents thirty years.

AGATE

عقيق

Agate is another popular mineral used as a gemstone which appears in strung bead form in Bedouin jewellery. The name "agate" is derived from the Greek Achates, a small rivulet in Sicily where it was extricated by ancient Greeks and Romans. Agate is also known as *aqiq*, which is the generic term for semi-precious stone. Distinguished by irregular bands of colour, agate is no exception as a subject for the counterfeiter. But imitations appear only occasionally in Bedouin jewellery, since genuine agate is readily available from many sources.

Agate is a chalcedony, and falls into the crypto-crystalline or fine-grained section. Agates include any chalcedony which displays a pattern, usually in bands and circles. It is formed by seeping water which carries silica, a whitish material, into holes and cracks in the rocks. The silica remains, piling up layer upon layer through the ages until it becomes agate: the different colours appear when the water picks up other minerals with the silica.

The gemstone can be coloured quite easily, and often the uninteresting coloured agate is dyed by jewellers to bring out beautiful patterns. Methods of treating its colour were known to the Romans.

Note: Under the signs of the zodiac agate represents Gemini.

عقيق   *aqiq*
عقد   *iqd*
حرز   *hirz*

Agate beads of various shapes are worn in profusion in the southwestern and southern part of the Arabian Peninsula. There are also fakes and these are equally popular but cost much less. A tribal woman prizes her agates, even if they do not have gilded silver granulated beads strung between. Such beads are prevalent in these regions and appear as part of necklaces that feature red and blue beads, sometimes in the form of coral and turquoise amongst agates.

The most desirable agate bead is the "teardrop" shape and these, too, are often imitated in glass and plastic.

It is not known if the agate used in Arabia in times past came from the Peninsula but, certainly today, they are imported and occasionally sold in bulk strands in local market places, suggesting that they arrive from India with other merchandise. This makes old agate necklaces precious and sought after.

GLASS & FAIENCE

زجاج و خزف مزخرف

Glass is a substance which is both hard and brittle, and can be either transparent or opaque. People who collect fine glass and all who admire it consider this invention one of the most exciting discoveries. Yet, how rarely do people trouble to think about so familiar a material. Strangely enough, glass experts still do not understand completely how it was first made, nor is it known exactly where or when. But almost certainly it was an accident.

The origin of glass [*zujaj*] was, according to tradition, the chance discovery of a group of ship-wrecked Phoenician sailors, when lighting a fire on a sandy beach. They are supposed to have noticed a vitreous material forming among the embers. There is possibly an element of truth in this myth, for the basic component of glass is sand [silica] which is fused with an alkaline substance [soda] and lime [calcium carbonate]. Furthermore, in the earliest days, the soda for glass-making was taken from seaweed or coastal plants which grows in abundance at the mouths of Eastern Mediterranean rivers. Glass has been known since the mid-second millennium BC. It is generally agreed that glass crafts began in one of the countries of the Eastern Mediterranean region. Although the earliest surviving examples have been discovered in Egypt, it is thought that the art reached there from Asia Minor. Both the ancient Egyptians and the Phoenicians traded in primitive glass ornaments. At first, glass was used to make ornaments. It was possible to colour glass pastes and apply them to small objects to make them look like precious stones. The paste could also be dripped into terracotta moulds to form small statues, plaques and jewellery components. To make hollow objects, the paste was placed around moulds which could afterwards be broken. This primitive glass paste was sometimes cut up into tiny pieces which were pierced and then strung together. Larger objects could not be made until the glass-makers were able to practise glass-blowing, which is believed to have been developed in Syria at the beginning of the Christian era. It is recorded that this great advance in glass-making was also an accident, occurring when an unnamed experimenter dipped one end of an iron tube into a pot of molten glass and blew down the tube. The resulting glass bubble was the beginning of bottles and other hollow glass vessels.

Faience [*khazaf muzakhraf*] the forerunner of glass, is a glazed pottery, the fused mixture of sand and lime covered with an alkaline glaze and it was an achievement of the ancient Egyptians. With both mediums, Egyptians were able to imitate coloured gems at relatively low cost. Glass, faience and substitute gems when used in imitation of a gem, are known as "paste" in English but something of this nature is called *taqleed* in Arabic.

Despite the fragility of glass, many beautiful ancient glass objects have been preserved. Superb glassware has been made in Czechoslovakia and fine examples of modern designs are made today in Scandinavia, while more classical pieces are reproduced in Italy, commanding very high prices. It is therefore peculiar that glass jewellery no longer receives the same respect it has in the past, although it may in time enjoy revived popularity, as have, for example, wooden beads.

For the Arabian Bedouin, the colours red and blue for set stones and strung beads, are far more important than whether glass and faience are used instead of garnet, carnelian, coral and turquoise.

زجاج	*zujaj*
خزف مزخرف	*khazaf musakhraf*
تقليد	*taqleed*
علاقة	*'laqah*

Coloured glass imitating gems is commonly incorporated into Bedouin jewellery, and it is also used for beads. In only one instance does it appear as mirror set in silver, as it is here in the Taifi medallion. This very rare necklace is unique to Saudi Arabia's mountaintop retreat for the well-to-do: Taif, set at the northern end of the Sarawat range in the southern part of Western Arabia, the Hijaz. Taif is also famous for its fruit and flowers.

The body of the ornament is formed with superb filigree and this is overlaid with applied decoration, including collets as beds for the tiny mirrors. The pendant charms are also set with mirror, as are the diamond-shaped beads which form part of the attractive chain.

Taifi medallions vary in size and quality, but they are always recognizable. Because their form and decoration are traditional they closely resemble each other.

BEADS

خرز

In the history of man, beads [*Khoraz*] have been important whether made from flint, drilled seeds, bone, teeth, claws, tusk, shells, wood or gem material. Beads have been used in tribal diplomacy as peace tokens, for barter and for currency; but primarily beads have been worn for decoration. Early men and women wore beads made of wood, a fashion which is popular again today.

Egyptian wall paintings of the Middle Kingdom, 2040–1730 BC and the New Kingdom 1500–900 BC, depict men drilling stone with bow drills to make beads. Even the poorest Egyptian of these times owned some kind of bead necklace.

Beads of jade, amber, coral, carnelian, feldspar, lapis lazuli, bronze, ceramic, glass and faience have been found together with tiny fragments of ancient glass on the surface of archaeological sites in the Eastern Province of Arabia, providing evidence of the Peninsula's bygone trade in beads from afar; for jade, lapis lazuli and bronze beads do not now appear in Arabian traditional Bedouin jewellery.

Together with costly frankincense and myrrh, beads, real and fake, are known to have been carried along the ancient trade routes.

Colourful beads, strung or pendant, are a common design element of Bedouin jewellery, just as they were in ancient Egypt. Like the Pharaohs, the Arabian Bedouin appreciate glass and faience.

Evidence of ancient bead-making, in the form of three manufacturing stages of fine glassy red and brown flint beads was found at historic Tayma – an important northern Arabian oasis town at the centre of an ancient trading network.

With their invention of glazed pottery faience and their glass-making skills, the Egyptians were able to imitate a diversity of coloured gems, becoming expert at their manufacture.

The actual source of Bedouin beads is difficult to ascertain since most necklaces have been rethreaded many times and the beads are often very old. Characteristic of Bedouin necklaces is the combination of beads of varying colour and size to form the major part of the strand, with larger beads and pendants occurring now and again in uniform relief. Graduated strands are unknown, and simple uniform strands of beads are uncommon.

Multi-stranded coral, and sometimes pearls, with relief beads at intervals, are occasionally seen, especially in Western Arabia but they are possibly a style brought in during the nineteenth century.

The relief beads in Arabian Bedouin jewellery are invariably silver. Sometimes as large as two inches in diameter. They are formed in two halves by the technique of embossing prior to being embellished and soldered together. Small silver beads and mace-shaped terminal beads made of silver are usually fashioned from pieces of metal folded over to meet, rather than solid drilled silver, as the former is lighter and the more economical method of production. Other shapes in silver beads include annular, bulbous, cylindrical and spherical. The richly embroidered, colourful Bedouin gowns are usually embellished with tiny silver "seed" beads and silver balls.

The link between Bedouin traditional jewellery and the ornamentation of ancient civilizations can be shown by means of beads. The identical mace-shaped bead which is commonly used in terminal position in Bedouin jewellery was used in the same position in Greek necklaces dated from the fourth century BC, and again appeared at the Jawan Tomb excavation in the Peninsula, dated about 100 AD. The cowrie shell-shaped bead also found in the Jawan Tomb was peculiar to Egyptian necklaces and girdles of the Middle Kingdom, when it was regarded as a fertility symbol and protective amulet for pregnant women. Cowrie shells from the Red Sea or Arabian Gulf were also common to necklaces worn about 5000 BC.

A very special necklace from western and south-western Arabia features fish, [*samak*] a fertility symbol since ancient times throughout the Middle East. This rare traditional necklace is often gold-washed. The example shown here appears to have its original threading, although it is possible some beads have been removed, as the fish are formed from very thin fine silver, and are occasionally flattened and broken. They alternate with silver beads, occasionally interspersed with a blue bead and sometimes a green bead, the latter inclusion peculiar to the Hijaz. Blue beads were included, it is said, to repel the Evil Eye.

خرز   *kharaz*
بدر   *badr*

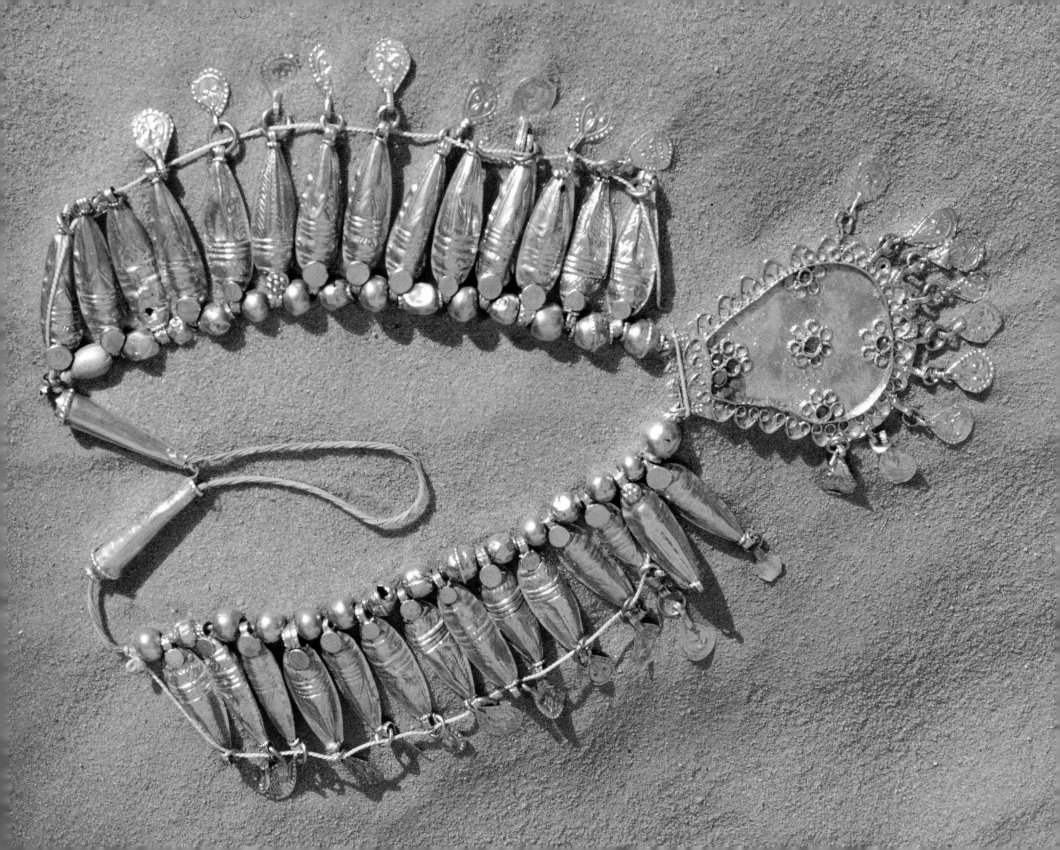

COINS

While Arabian Bedouin jewellery closely resembles that of long dead civilizations, a decorative dimension of its very own is added, in the form of coins [*umla*] used plain or embellished in rings and as pendants.

On the Arabian Peninsula, the most common *umla* used in Bedouin jewellery is the Maria Theresa thaler, often highly decorated with beads and bells. These large silver coins of the Austro-Hungarian empire [but minted in London] all bear the mint date of 1780. Until recently they were official tender in Yemen and used as currency in surrounding regions. The thaler is, in fact, still being minted for use in some countries, and there are also many counterfeits of silver content lower than the authentic 80 per cent pure thalers.

When coins were first invented, they were worth their weight in whatever metal they were made of; today they are rarely more than tokens. Their function, however, has remained the same.

The earliest coins, taking the place of barter, were crudely fashioned pieces of metal. Earlier than actual coinage, the ancient Egyptians and peoples of Mesopotamia were in fact using precious metals: gold, silver, electrum [the natural amalgam of silver and gold], and bronze, which were weighed for the purpose of estimating value.

Coins, writes Howard Linecar, evolved simply from the various pieces of metal used in barter to blobs of a certain metal of a stipulated weight bearing the sign of a particular merchant. His mark guaranteed the metal's worth.

On this method grew the whole system of exchange by money. It is believed that an Ionian merchant first thought of impressing on a lump of gold a mark with a sharp tool which he was able to recognize when it once more passed through his hands. And, it is recorded that the King of Lydia, who, seeing the merchants' marks, began to mark his own gold coins with the royal seal. This was circa 665 bc. The coins of King Croesus of Lydia in the following century are the most famous of the ancient world.

The first coin issued by the Saudi Arabian Government in 1925, was a copper and nickel coin called a "qirsh", minted in the name of Abd al-Aziz ibn Saud as "King of the Hejaz and Sultan of Najd." Other coins in circulation in the area included the British gold sovereign, the gold Trans-Jordanian dinar, the Indian rupee, the Maria Theresa thaler and the Turkish silver majeedi – the last three most commonly found in Bedouin jewellery. Indian currency was used in Oman, in the south of the Arabian Peninsula.

In 1928, Saudi Arabia established a bi-metallic independent monetary system of its own, based on the silver riyal using the British gold sovereign as its standard base, with a value of one sovereign to ten riyals. The riyal was divided into twenty-two "qirsh darij". The all-metal currency commanded the confidence of the people who traditionally relied on the intrinsic metal content of money. Fluctuations in the values of the two currencies and a strong feeling held by the religious authorities that Islamic law forbade coins to circulate at a value above that of their metallic value content, made it necessary to use full weight silver riyals. Any significant rise in the world price of silver made it profitable to export the riyal or melt it down for use as silver bullion. For this reason, in 1935, the new silver riyal of smaller weight and size was struck. At the same time, a new silver half-riyal and quarter-riyal coins were issued. None have been minted since 1955, and since the value of their silver content exceeds their value as coins, they are difficult to find. However, all of these silver coins can be found as component parts of Bedouin jewellery, albeit defaced and with the detail often obliterated with decoration and/or wear.

A variety of *umla* have been used as components of Bedouin jewellery and perhaps the most interesting is the British Trade Dollar, a silver coin issued between 1895 and 1935 to promote British commerce in the East. These dollars had been requested for many years by local bankers and merchants, who eventually paid for the costs of their production. Jewellery coins are more often Maria Theresa thalers, sometimes so encrusted with beads and ornamentation that they are recognizable only from the back. Other coins include Egyptian, minted in the twenties in the time of Sultan Fuad, the father of King Farouk, and various early Saudi coins of high silver content.

This necklace of large granulated silver and fake amber beads, supports a sealed silver charm case with coin pendants. Two are Saudi Arabian and one is English.

عملة *umla*

APPENDIX 1

Gemstones

Most precious stones are minerals but out of approximately three thousand kinds of mineral stones only about seventy have ever been regarded as gemstones. These, however, have remained popular for thousands of years.

Initially it may have been the colour of gemstones which attracted primitive man, yet we know from research that specific properties and characteristics eventually led them to be highly valued. Perhaps in earliest times gemstones were used purely for adornment at first; later, certainly, they were acquired for religious and superstitious purposes as well. In time they became valued for dynastic purposes as Crown Jewels, and curses were often attributed to great stones. In medicine too they found a place, and they were also associated with astrology. Today, precious stones are applied in technology and worn as birthstones.

Like anything else of value, precious stones have been copied. The history of imitation and fake gems is long and it can be seen that jewel substitutes were used by the Egyptians, Greeks, Romans and Phoenicians but not as efficiently as they are today. There are ways to detect imitations, but the only sure method is to remove the stone from its setting and put it to the test prescribed by gemology for the analysis of that particular gem. However, a keen eye, together with some basic knowledge, will sometimes give a correct answer. Such can be the case with a "jeweller" who is rarely a gemologist. The gemologist's science is concerned with investigating and establishing facts about gems and gemstones since they are of monetary value and proper identification is crucial. The laws and procedures applied to the study of minerals fit gemstones perfectly so any trained mineralogist can soon become a competent gemologist. In analysis of gems and jewels, the chemical composition, internal structure, light characteristics, and other physical characteristics such as hardness, are the important factors to be considered.

Confusion has arisen on occasions in the basic vocabulary within the subject of gemology. Paul Desautels, Curator of Gems and Minerals for the Smithsonian Institution writes: "'Gemstones' are the specially treasured minerals found in the earth and 'gems' are the objects fashioned from them; 'jewels' are gems that have been prepared for mounting in jewellery or other works of art." However, in history, a "jewel" could have been any small piece of jewellery with or without a set gem.

Jewels, like potatoes are measured by weight. The basic unit is a carat, a word derived from "carob", a small Oriental bean remarkable for its uniformity of size, once used in weighing gems. A carat is 1/142nd of an avoirdupois ounce or 200 milligrams. The carat weight is often described another way; as one fifth of a metric gramme, subdivided into 100 points.

From archaeological evidence the existence of the gem trade routes has been traced to a pre-dynastic period, well before 5,000 BC. In these researches certain non-minerals – coral, pearl, jet and ivory – join the organic compound, amber, to become an accepted part of the earth's treasury of gems.

Jade and lapis lazuli beads have been found on the ancient sites in the Arabian Peninsula, but they are no longer used in Arabian body ornament. Amber, coral, garnet and turquoise, in contrast, have remained popular for two thousand years there.

The tendency to attribute certain stones with powers was often the reason for a specific selection. For example, green stones were believed by the ancients to prevent disease whilst red stones were reserved for the alleviation of bleeding and inflammation; agate was worn to make the wearer agreeable and more persuasive, amethyst was chosen to ward off intoxication, coral for wisdom, and malachite was used as a local anaesthetic or worn as protection against malign enchantment. Sapphire the emblem of chastity, often chosen as an alternative "engagement" gem to the diamond, the symbol of "eternity", was once considered to be a cure for boils. The practice of relating a gemstone to the birth month of the wearer is relatively recent, having been introduced sometime in the eighteenth century. An individual could change ornaments each month, thereby receiving the virtues of all the stones, but gradually, the emphasis changed to wearing one stone, representing the birth month of the wearer, thus bestowing an extra measure of its virtues upon him.

Man still pays economic homage to these old traditions.

APPENDIX 2

Middle Eastern Mining

A.J. Wilson has written in *Optima*: "It is no more possible to say with certainty when and where copper mining and smelting first started on earth than it is to date precisely the end of the Bronze Age or the beginning of the Iron Age. Of Timna, the most cautious archaeologist and historian are agreed that here, and in its adjoining valleys, copper mining has already spanned some six thousand years."

Gus van Beek, Curator of the Old World Archaeology at the Smithsonian Institution writes in *The Rise and Fall of Arabia Felix*, that brass objects first appeared in southern Arabia in the first century BC, with some certainly imported, but others probably made locally.

Historically, brass was an alloy of copper with zinc and tin, bronze being copper and tin only. Today, this yellow alloy is usually copper with zinc only, a third of the total weight being zinc.

Sources of copper in the past were within the Peninsula, and to the north at the head of the Gulf of Aqaba. There has long been speculation about the location of the fabled mines of King Solomon and the search for them has led to a confirmation of several ancient workings of rich copper deposits. Since 1845 a site named Timna in the Wadi Arabah, thirty miles north of Elat, at the head of the Gulf of Aqaba, has been regarded as a major site. Timna is a proven source of ancient mineral wealth, especially copper.

On the assumption that the fabled mines had been located, one of the most impressive of the many groups of majestic red sandstone formations which dominate the valley was named King Solomon's Pillars. But since 1964, this has been refuted as investigations have established that there is nothing to identify Timna with King Solomon's mines.

This does not mean that the copper used to make the brass for Arabian jewellery did not come from Timna, but it is more likely that it came from within the Arabian Peninsula.

Within Arabia, mineral books record Samrah in Central Arabia as a source of silver. The metal has also been located in the West, and in the southern and eastern shields. Samrah's mines ceased operation in about 800 AD. The most exciting find came in the 1930s, when the American engineer Twitchell was invited to Arabia to investigate the country's water potential. During the visit, he saw a bag of rocks from Western Arabia which appeared to be rich mineral ore. Upon assay Twitchell confirmed that this ore was indeed incredibly rich and subsequent mining by the Saudi Arabian Mining Syndicate [SAMS] between 1939 and 1954 recorded production of 765,768 fine ounces of gold and 1,002,029 ounces of silver.

The United States Department of the Interior's Geological Survey Report of 1975 on Geology and Ore Deposits of the Mahd Adh Dhahab District, Kingdom of Saudi Arabia, prepared for the Directorate General of Mineral Resources, Ministry of Petroleum and Mineral Resources, written by Robert W. Luce, Abdulaziz Bagdady, and Ralph J. Roberts, states that this area is the most productive within the Kingdom. The name of the source of precious metal, Mahd Adh Dhahab, means "Cradle of Gold," which could be freely translated as Mother Lode.

The radiocarbon method of dating known as "carbon 14" was used on slag at Mahd Adh Dhahab's ancient mining sites, indicating that the mines were functioning during two distinct periods in the Peninsula's early history. Carbon from the older slag indicated a date of about 3,000 years ago, whereas carbon from other slag suggested a date of about 1,000 years ago.

No records of production are available for these early operations, but when SAMS began mining there in 1939, it was estimated that nearly 1,000,000 short tons of tailings and dumps were piled around the workings. About 293,848 tons of these discards were later treated by SAMS and yielded about 0.62 ounces of gold per ton, so it is inferred that higher grade material was treated in the ancient mines. The early miners had worked to a depth of 85 metres and recent investigations indicated further rich ore deeper underground.

Some of the silver in Arabian Bedouin jewellery could have come from Madh Adh Dhahab. It might perhaps be proven if any ornaments still existed which were several hundred years old. This is most improbable but it is feasible that the older pieces contain a proportion of silver from ancient yields.

Gold has now been discovered at some six hundred sites within the Kingdom of Saudi Arabia; and, in addition to vast oil and gas reserves, a wealth of other metallic and industrial minerals lie still largely unexploited.

APPENDIX 3

Gem Classification

Some of the best gem study techniques unfortunately involve destruction of the sample. Therefore, destructive tests are generally reserved for uncut gemstones. Among such tests are chemical analysis, X-ray structure determination, and Mohs' tests for hardness. Non-destructive tests include determination of refractive index; specific gravity; pleochroism; spectral pattern; and examination for any foreign inclusions in the stone. These tests are usually adequate for correct analysis.

Refractive index
As a beam of light hits the flat surface of a mineral at an angle, it bends (or refracts) upon entering the gem. If the light beam's direction is slowly changed so that it comes to the surface of the gem at an increasingly lower angle, eventually a point is reached where it ceases to bend sufficiently to enter the gem. It just grazes the surface. Any further lowering of the beam causes it to be totally reflected away from the gem. The grazing angle is called the "critical angle", and it will differ with each gem substance according to its refracting ability.

An instrument, the gem refractometer, has been devised to measure this "critical angle" quickly and easily. The instrument usually contains a built-in scale from which the refracting ability, or "refractive index", of the gem can be read. To read the index on a typical gem refractometer, one of the polished facets of the gem is placed against a polished piece of very highly refracting glass mounted in the instrument. Good contact is assured by placing a drop of highly refracting liquid between them. A light beam is brought through the glass to the gem. Any of the light coming to the gem from an angle at which it will be refracted is bent into the gem, away from the instrument and is lost. Light coming in at any angle beyond the critical is reflected back into the instrument, hits the viewing eyepiece, and its trace shows as a bright section on the scale. The numerical marking on the scale dividing the light portion – representing reflected light – and the dark portion – representing the lost light refracted into the gem – is the critical angle. For convenience, this is numbered on the scale as the refractive index. The measurement is sufficiently precise so that, by consulting a table listing the refractive indices of gemstones, one can usually make a quick identification of the gem in question.

Specific Gravity
Specific gravity is the weight of a gem compared with the weight of an equal volume of water. To determine specific gravity of a gem, is to weigh it accurately in air and weigh it again while it is immersed in water. The "in water" weight is subtracted from the "in air" weight. This gives the weight of a volume of water equal to the volume of the gem. This weight is divided into the weight of the gem in air to find how many times it exceeds the weight of the water – thus its specific gravity.

Pleochroism
Different colours can often be observed in double refracting gems by looking at them from different directions. Any colour differences are recorded. This pleochroism or diochroism can be seen and the colours compared directly by using an instrument called a dichroscope.

Spectral Analysis
Spectral analysis for coloured gemstones can supply useful information for identification by use of the gem spectroscope. Its function is based on the separation of white light into its complete rainbow – or spectrum, of colours.

Gemstone Inclusions
Gemstones under magnification reveal an amazing myriad of inclusions – with from ten to forty times magnification under a microscope, it is possible not only to identify the gem because of its characteristic inclusions, but to learn exactly where in the world it came from. Inclusions are invariably present. Even the "perfect" diamond has inclusions but it is ranked "perfect" if no inclusions are apparent when magnified to ten times.

X-Ray
Although the kind of X-ray examination of most value to gemology requires the destruction of a small amount of the stone, it remains the most important single key to identification.

However, as mineralogists and gemologists have assembled sufficient instruments and non-destructive techniques, destructive analysis is a last

APPENDIX 4

resort. Rarely can gem material perplex an expert. Yet, science is also perfecting the ability to manufacture gemstones, so it is obvious that gemology must be kept to a strict thoroughness if the distinctions between natural and man-made gems are not to be obscured.

Care of jewellery

The diamond, as the hardest of gemstones, is the most impervious to damage but care must be taken to protect the setting or the stone may be lost. In all cases, jewellery should be treated as something treasured and delicate. Individual pieces should be kept in individual containers and these should be lined with a soft material.

Gemstones are classified on a hardness scale, the softest quickly losing beauty when scratched or cracked. The most precious gemstone is often considered to be emerald which is one of the more easily damaged gems.

One of the best ways to think of hardness is as the scratch-resisting ability of the gem. Since the early 1800s, a rough but convenient scale for measuring hardness [originated by the German mineralogist Friedrich Mohs] has been in general use. The Mohs scale is based on ten relatively common minerals ranked from l to 10 in order of increasing hardness:

1	talc	6	feldspar
2	gypsum	7	quartz
3	calcite	8	topaz
4	fluorite	9	corundum
5	apatite	10	diamond

The degree to which hardness increases between the numbers is not at all uniform. There is a greater degree of difference between the hardness of corundum and diamond – 9 and 10 in the scale – than between the numbers 1 and 9. Almost all important gemstones have a hardness above 6 in this scale. Gemstones do break,

sometimes from a blow and sometimes as a result of sudden and extreme cooling and heating.

Due to the conditions under which the Bedouin live, their jewellery has been subjected to excessive heat and dryness, abrasive dust and the body's acidic moisture, all of which tend to damage the ornaments. Professional cleaning at regular intervals is recommended for jewellery generally, but home care, painstakingly carried out, can suffice.

The mildest effective cleaning abrasive for jewellery is toothpaste, applied with a very soft natural bristle brush.

Silver polish is not ideal for intricate Bedouin jewellery as any residue retained in the intricately embellished surfaces spoils the appearance of the jewellery. Liquid silver dip is probably the most effective way of removing damaging tarnish from such surfaces. The danger is leaving the metal in the liquid too long or perhaps not rinsing the item enough.

Dishwashing liquid soap and water are excellent for restoring gold to brightness and also essential after liquid cleaning of silver. The best method of preserving the brightness of silver once cleaned, is to keep it from the air to prevent the everpresent oxides from setting up the tarnishing process once again.

It is a matter of preference, however, whether to keep Bedouin jewellery highly polished or merely clean. The best silver pieces of almost pure silver content, respond well to soap and water followed by burnishing with a soft cloth.

APPENDIX 5

The Women's Suq

The Women's *Suq* in Riyadh was a colourful market which was run entirely by women and for years remained a favourite haunt of expatriate residents and visitors to the capital. Originally this *suq* sold new and used clothing as well as herbs, spices and an assortment of cooking utensils. Later, the women traders also kept large collections of old silver jewellery and some old gold ornaments. Many of the gold adornments were set with Gulf pearls. The more modern gold pieces displayed cultured pearls from Japan, as pearl-fishing in the Arabian Gulf and Red Sea is rarely practised today, partly because of the ready availability of Japanese pearls.

Most of the jewellery shown in this book was purchased in Riyadh, where the two large market areas are the Dira and Batha *suqs*. The Women's *Suq* was within the Dira area and the older and more desirable silver jewellery was to be found there, surprisingly cheaper than the new pieces sold by the silversmiths working in an area at the rear of the Batha *Suq*. The rising cost of labour and materials was probably the reason for the disparity in price .

The "Antiques" *Suq*, also within Dira, has Kuwaiti and Medina chests; occasionally a pearling chest with its many small compartments; incense burners; wooden camel's milk bowls; copper pans; brass coffee pots; brass and wooden mortars and pestles; coffee bean roasters; swords; daggers; guns; suits of chain mail and many other interesting ethnic items which includes Bedouin jewellery.

In these *suqs*, as throughout the Middle

East, bargaining is an acceptable and expected procedure. A single bracelet instead of a pair, or an imperfection and a little damage, will rarely affect the price. Rather, it would seem, the *rapport* which can be built up between the buyer and the seller, or sometimes the heat and the time of day or year, will do so. Shoppers bargain for almost everything in the *suqs* and Westeners spend hours haggling there. Bargaining can add zest to a mundane shopping chore and once experienced in it, most people enjoy participating in a good-natured exchange over a price. "Getting a bargain" is always satisfying. One felt, too, that the Bedouin traders in the Women's *Suq* enjoyed the exchange with foreign customers as much as they liked concluding a sale. This foreign interest has naturally caused a sharp rise in the price of all ethnic items and has resulted in a scarcity of traditional jewellery.

As the Government of Saudi Arabia has established a Department of Antiquities, which enforces regulations pertaining to the export of antiquities and ethnic items, it is wise to consult the Department's representative in Riyadh, Jiddah, Madinah, Dammam or Abha before making any sizeable purchase. This Department has the right to judge individual cases on their merits and consider whether the export of any item would improverish the Kingdom's archaeological, artistic or historical heritage. Eventually many of such pieces will be exhibited in Saudi Arabia's local museums. Anyone who truly appreciates these aspects of the Arabian heritage should abide by these rules.

Most foreigners in Saudi Arabia endeavour to acquire a basic Arabic vocabulary, but few achieve fluency. However, experience shows that fluent Arabic is not essential for shopping in the *suqs*, although it is wise to learn the words which relate to any specific field of interest, and to have a good idea of the currency and values before venturing forth. Courteous greetings and farewells are appreciated by the Bedouin women traders and to count in Arabic is an obvious advantage.

In comparison with the other *suqs* in Riyadh, the Women's *Suq* was a quiet place, perhaps noticeably so because of the large crowds in the Meat and Vegetable *Suqs* directly in front. It aroused a sense of excitement in foreign visitors seeking Bedouin jewellery to pass through the entrance to the Women's *Suq*, where eggs were sold, despite the fact that they may have visited there many times before. It was a unique sight. The stalls displayed a fascinating variety: colourful and pungent spices, brilliant-hued dresses, old and new; cooking utensils and ingredients; and Bedouin silver jewellery. And, there was an unmistakable air of expectancy among the stall-holders .

Sometimes it is difficult for Westerners to restrain showing eagerness but it is an important part of the bargaining ritual to feign indifference.

The shelters of wood and corrugated iron gave shade to these Bedouin women traders, who wore traditional brightly–coloured, full-length, long-sleeved dresses partly covered by black cloaks [*abayat*]. Their greetings were friendly, as they

invited a customer to sit on the ground with them to examine their wares and do some quiet browsing and haggling. Squatting on a piece of carpet, surrounded by the dish containing a profusion of silver turquoise-studded jewellery with beads of red coral, blue faience, brown agate and golden amber and silver, hanging like colourful screens – with the elaborate Bedouin garments spilling forth from the cavernous chests at the back – made it difficult to make a choice.

The most costly pieces of jewellery were kept in closed showcases or in small tin containers, which were brought out only if requested or if the stall-holder considered that she might have a good sale in the offing.

It was fascinating to learn from these women that this jewellery often came from far away, crafted in many towns and cities of Arabia, and sometimes in other Middle Eastern countries; and that a nomadic Bedouin woman wore and enjoyed these ornaments for a lifetime in the desert until, no less valued, they appeared for sale in the capital city of Saudi Arabia.

APPENDIX 6   The influence of Arab and Related Cultures

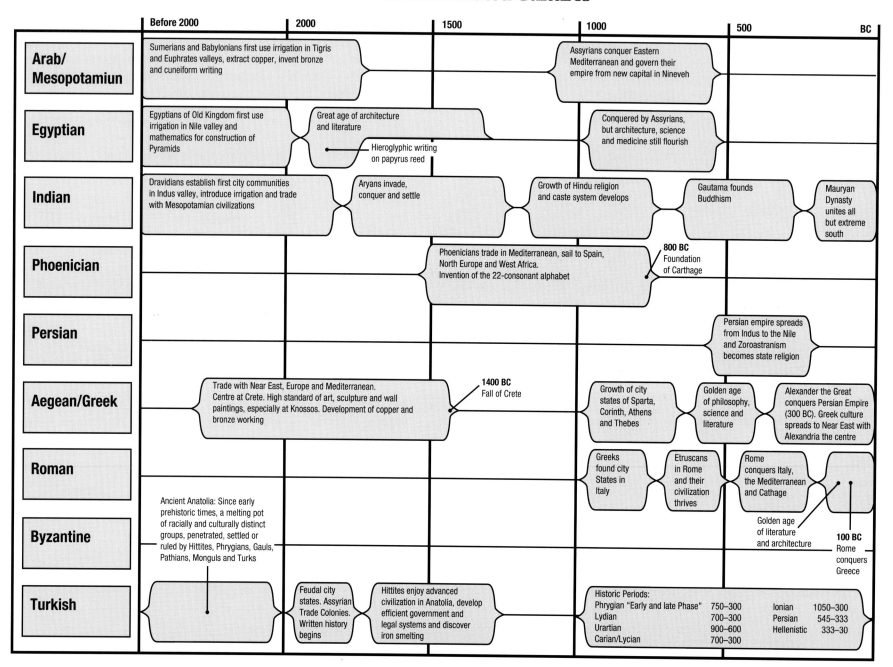

	Before 2000	2000	1500	1000	500	BC

Arab/Mesopotamiun
Sumerians and Babylonians first use irrigation in Tigris and Euphrates valleys, extract copper, invent bronze and cuneiform writing

Assyrians conquer Eastern Mediterranean and govern their empire from new capital in Nineveh

Egyptian
Egyptians of Old Kingdom first use irrigation in Nile valley and mathematics for construction of Pyramids

Great age of architecture and literature

Hieroglyphic writing on papyrus reed

Conquered by Assyrians, but architecture, science and medicine still flourish

Indian
Dravidians establish first city communities in Indus valley, introduce irrigation and trade with Mesopotamian civilizations

Aryans invade, conquer and settle

Growth of Hindu religion and caste system develops

Gautama founds Buddhism

Mauryan Dynasty unites all but extreme south

Phoenician
Phoenicians trade in Mediterranean, sail to Spain, North Europe and West Africa. Invention of the 22-consonant alphabet

800 BC Foundation of Carthage

Persian
Persian empire spreads from Indus to the Nile and Zoroastranism becomes state religion

Aegean/Greek
Trade with Near East, Europe and Mediterranean. Centre at Crete. High standard of art, sculpture and wall paintings, especially at Knossos. Development of copper and bronze working

1400 BC Fall of Crete

Growth of city states of Sparta, Corinth, Athens and Thebes

Golden age of philosophy, science and literature

Alexander the Great conquers Persian Empire (300 BC). Greek culture spreads to Near East with Alexandria the centre

Roman
Greeks found city States in Italy

Etruscans in Rome and their civilization thrives

Rome conquers Italy, the Mediterranean and Cathage

Golden age of literature and architecture

100 BC Rome conquers Greece

Byzantine
Ancient Anatolia: Since early prehistoric times, a melting pot of racially and culturally distinct groups, penetrated, settled or ruled by Hittites, Phrygians, Gauls, Pathians, Monguls and Turks

Turkish
Feudal city states. Assyrian Trade Colonies. Written history begins

Hittites enjoy advanced civilization in Anatolia, develop efficient government and legal systems and discover iron smelting

Historic Periods:
Phrygian "Early and late Phase"	750–300	Ionian	1050–300
Lydian	700–300	Persian	545–333
Urartian	900–600	Hellenistic	333–30
Carian/Lycian	700–300		

120

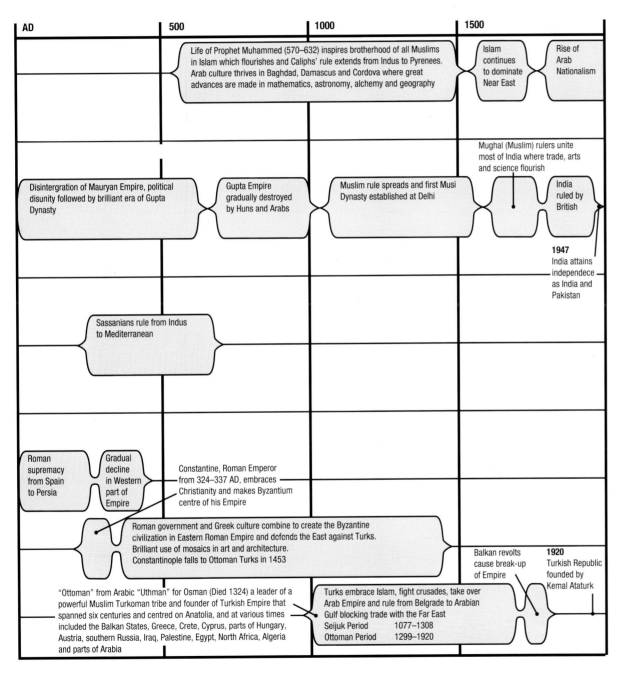

AD	500	1000	1500

Life of Prophet Muhammed (570–632) inspires brotherhood of all Muslims in Islam which flourishes and Caliphs' rule extends from Indus to Pyrenees. Arab culture thrives in Baghdad, Damascus and Cordova where great advances are made in mathematics, astronomy, alchemy and geography

Islam continues to dominate Near East

Rise of Arab Nationalism

Mughal (Muslim) rulers unite most of India where trade, arts and science flourish

Disintergration of Mauryan Empire, political disunity followed by brilliant era of Gupta Dynasty

Gupta Empire gradually destroyed by Huns and Arabs

Muslim rule spreads and first Musi Dynasty established at Delhi

India ruled by British

1947 India attains independece as India and Pakistan

Sassanians rule from Indus to Mediterranean

Roman supremacy from Spain to Persia

Gradual decline in Western part of Empire

Constantine, Roman Emperor from 324–337 AD, embraces Christianity and makes Byzantium centre of his Empire

Roman government and Greek culture combine to create the Byzantine civilization in Eastern Roman Empire and defends the East against Turks. Brilliant use of mosaics in art and architecture. Constantinople falls to Ottoman Turks in 1453

Balkan revolts cause break-up of Empire

1920 Turkish Republic founded by Kemal Ataturk

"Ottoman" from Arabic "Uthman" for Osman (Died 1324) a leader of a powerful Muslim Turkoman tribe and founder of Turkish Empire that spanned six centuries and centred on Anatolia, and at various times included the Balkan States, Greece, Crete, Cyprus, parts of Hungary, Austria, southern Russia, Iraq, Palestine, Egypt, North Africa, Algeria and parts of Arabia

Turks embrace Islam, fight crusades, take over Arab Empire and rule from Belgrade to Arabian Gulf blocking trade with the Far East
Seijuk Period 1077–1308
Ottoman Period 1299–1920

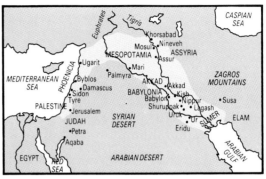

The Fertile Crescent

The fertile band of land which horseshoes north, then west, then south is a semi-circle westward from the Arabian Gulf to the Mediterranean, is generally referred to as the Fertile Crescent. In ancient times, its geographic position and fecundity made it a magnet to peoples from the surrounding areas, to wandering Semitic tribes from the Arabian deserts and to non-Semite peoples from the mountainous North.

The part of the horseshoe which first attracted settlers was the eastern side to the north of the Arabian Gulf, between the Tigris and Euphrates Rivers, and known in history primarily as Mesopotamia. Later, the western side, along the Mediterranean coast, also drew many immigrants.

Not without reason did it become known as the Cradle of Civilization. Some of the most important cultural and technical advances of the ancient world were made there.

The Mesopotamian civilization could be considered never really to have died, for each successive dynasty built upon those that preceded it.

121

BIBLIOGRAPHY

The following list comprises the sources that I have consulted and found illuminating, but it does not include the numerous Middle Eastern journals and periodicals which provided so much information, mainly pictorial, in regard to the wearing of traditional Bedouin jewellery.

Al-Farsy, Fouad, Modernity and Tradition – The Saudi Equation, Knight Communications Ltd., Guernsey, Channel Islands, 1994

Antiquities and Museums, Department of Ministry of Education, Riyadh, Kingdom of Saudi Arabia, Atlal, Vol. 1. 1977 – Vol. 13. 1990

Aramco Handbook, The Arabian American Oil Company (Dhahran), 1960

Aramco World Magazine, article entitled "Crusaders", Vol. 21, No. 3, May/June 1970

Area Handbook for Saudi Arabia, Foreign Area Studies, The American University, Washington, 1966

Argenzio, Victor *Fascination of Diamonds*, George Allen and Unwin Limited, London 1966

Assah, Ahmed *Miracle of a Desert Kingdom,* Johnson Publications Limited, London, 1969

d'Aulaire, Emily and Perola Article entitled "Gold of the North" in *Scanorama*, Scandinavian Airlines magazine, NAG Press Limited

Basil, Malin *Arabia Through the Eyes of an Artist*, Falcon Press, 1977

Baumgartel, Elise J. *The Cultures of Prehistoric Egypt: Part II Silver*, Oxford University Press for The Griffith Institute, 1960

Bibby, Geoffrey *Looking For Dilmun*, Alfred Knopf Inc, New York, 1970

British Museum Publications Limited *Jewellery Through 7000 Years*, 1976

Desautels, Paul E. *Gem Kingdom*, The Smithsonian Institution, Ridge Press, Random House Inc, New York

Dickson, H.R.P. *Arab of the Desert*, George Allen and Unwin Limited, London, 1952

Fletcher, Lucinda *Silver*, Orbis Publishing Limited, London, 1975

Ghantus, Leila Article entitled "The Music of Arabia" from *Ahlan Wasahlan*, Issue No. 2, Vol. 1, October/November/December 1977, Saudi Arabian Airlines Corporation

Gordus, Adon and Jeanne Article entitled "There's Gold in Them Thar Coins", *LSA*, Spring 1977, University of Michigan publication

Hasson, Rachel *Early Islamic Jewellery*, L.A. Mayer Memorial Institute for Islamic Art 1987

Hasson, Rachel *Later Islamic Jewellery*, L.A. Mayer Memorial Institute for Islamic Art 1987

Hinks, Peter *Jewellery*, The Hamlyn Publishing Group Limited, London 1969

Katakura, Motoko *Bedouin Village*, University of Tokyo Press, 1977

Khuri, Zahi Article entitled "Arabesque" from *Ahlan Wasahlan*, Issue No. 1, Vol. 2, January/February/March, 1978, Saudi Arabian Airlines Corporation

Linecar, Howard *Coins*, The Hamlyn Publishing Group Limited, London 1971

Luce, R.W., Bagdady Abdulaziz and Roberts, R.J. "Geology and Ore Deposits of the Mahd Adh Dhahab District" from *Saudi Arabian Project Reports*, (IR-201 and 106; IR-195), prepared for Director General of Mineral Resources, Ministry of Petroleum, Saudi Arabia 1975

Mariacher, Giovanni *Glass from Antiquity to the Renaissance*, The Hamlyn Publishing Group Limited, London 1970

McClure, H.A. *The Arabian Peninsula and Prehistoric Populations*, edited by Henry Field, Field Research Projects Study No. 58, 1972

Michaud, Sabrina and Roland Article entitled "Bold Horsemen of the Steppes" in *National Geographic Magazine*, November 1973

O'Neill, Thomas J. Article entitled "Amber, Golden Window on the Past", with photographs by Paul A. Zahl, Vol. 153, No. 3, *National Geographic Magazine*

Phillips, Wendell *Unknown Oman*, Longman Group Limited, London, 1971

Platt, Nathaniel and Drummond, Muriel Jean *Our World Through the Ages*, Prentice Hall Inc, New York, 1954

Readers Digest Great World Atlas, The Readers Digest Association Limited

Richards, Alison and Sataloff, Joseph *The Pleasure of Jewellery and Gemstones*, Octopus Books Limited, London, 1974

Tordoff, William *Ashanti Under the Prempehs 1888–1935*, Oxford University Press, 1965

US Military Area Handbook for Saudi Arabia, US Government Printing Office, Washington

Van Beek, Gus W. Article entitled "The Rise and Fall of Arabia Felix" in the *Scientific American*, W.H Freeman and Co, San Francisco

Verband der Edelstein und Diamanten-industrie *Edelsteine—Precious Stones*, Schaefer and Schmidt, Germany, 1966

Videl, F.S. *Pre-lslamic Burial Report*, English version of Arabic article published in Mecca monthly magazine, *Al Manhal*, (pp 546–553) Sha'ban 1375, April 1956

Webster, Robert *Gems*, Butterworth and Co. Limited, London, 1970

Weir, Shelagh *The Bedouin*, Museum of Mankind, UK World of Islam Festival Publishing Co. Limited, London 1976

Wills, Geoffrey *Glass*, Orbis Publishing Limited, London, 1975

Wilson, A.J. Article entitled "Timna's Ancient Mining Secrets" in *Optima*, a review published by the Anglo-American Corporation, De Beers and Charter Consolidated Groups of Companies

Further reading

Ross, Heather Colyer, *The Art of Bedouin Jewellery: A Saudi Arabian Profile*, Arabesque Commercial SA, PO Box 9 1815 Clarens–Montreux Switzerland, 1994.

Ross, Heather Colyer, *The Art of Arabian Costume: A Saudi Arabian Profile*, Arabesque Commercial SA, PO Box 9 1815 Clarens–Montreux Switzerland, 1994.

GLOSSARY OF ARABIC WORDS

abayah pl. *abayat*	traditional Arab cloak
Afriqi	African (adj)
ahjar hamra	red stones (as gems)
ahzimah	waistbelts
Al-Ajam	The Persians
Ajami	Persian (adj)
amal silsilah	chainmaking
anbar	combustible material (amber)
aqiq	agate
aqiq ahmar	carnelian
Al-Atrak	The Turks
Al-Badw	The Bedouin
Badawi	Bedouin (adj)
badr	full moon
buruz	repoussé
dabb	lizard
dhahab	gold
Al-Etruo	The Etruscans
Etruwi	Etruscan (adj)
fariuz	turquoise
fatkhah (pl. fatakh)	red stone ring
fawariz	rings
fiddah	silver
fraida	large nose ornament
habbiyat	granulation
hafr	engraving
Hajj	Muslim pilgrimage to Makkah
halaq	earring
hijab	small charms/rectangular-shaped amulet box
hijl (pl. hujul)	anklet
Hijiri	Muslim calendar, which dates from the
Hijrah	Prophet's migration from Makkah to Madinah 622 AD
hilal	crescent moon

hijiri	the Islamic calendar
hijrah	travel to/leave for another place
hilyat sha'r	hair ornament
hirz	amulet charm case
hizam (pl. ahzimah)	belt
Al-lghriq also *Younan*	The Greeks
Ighriqi also *Younani*	Greeks (adj.)
'ilaqah	headdress ornament
imam	a leader in prayer
iqd	necklace
jauharah	gemstone
jnad	large necklace worn under one arm
kaff	"glove" ornament
kaffat or khamasiyat	forehead ornament
kahraman	amber
khalifat	caliphs
khalkhal (pl. khalakhil)	anklet
khamzad	ring worn on little finger
kharaz	beads
kharaz al kabseh or *kharaz al akhdar*	green stones
kharaz al halib	white stones (as gems)
khatim (pl. khawatim)	ring
khazaf	pottery, china, ceramics
khazaf muzakhraf	faience
khiyarah	cylindrical-shaped amulet box
khizama	small nose ring
khurafah (pl. khumfat)	superstition
khurs (pl. khirsan)	earring
kirdala or kirdan	choker necklace
lazm	ornament worn under chin, from ear to ear
liham	soldered or soldering
lulu	pearl
ma sha la	according to God's will
madan mutarraz	wrought metal

mahfur	engraved or engraving
mahr	provision of dowry
majlis	council
al-marami	thin rings
marjan	coral
maskah or *samakah*	religious amulets
Al-Masriyyum	The Egyptians
Masri	Egyptian (adj)
mata'hin	coined and belled ring
mesbaha also *subha*	Islamic prayer-beads
milak	engagement contract
muakhkhar	second part of dowry, sum promised to wife in case of divorce
muqaddam	first part of dowry, payable on engagement
mushabbak	filgree
nahas asfar	brass
naqsh	chasing
Nepali	Nepalese (adj)
qat'jauharah	gemstone cutting
qiladah	pendant necklace
qimah	value
qirsh	copper and nickel Saudi coin
Ramadan	Muslim month of fasting
Al-Rum	The Byzantines
Rumi	Byzantine (adj)
Al-Ruman	The Romans
Rumani	Roman (adj)
sahr	fusing, fusion
saigh al dhahab	goldsmith
saigh al fiddah	silversmith
sakb	sandcasting
Al-Salibiyyum	The Crusaders
shaf	small nose ornament
shahadah	Islamic doctrinal formula
al-shahid	forefinger and thus ring worn on it
shaikh	religious scholar or tribal leader

Sharqi	Oriental (adj)
shugl al khurduq	granulation
silk	wire
silsilah	chain
Al-Siniyyun	The Chinese
Sini	Chinese (adj)
siwar (pl. asawir)	bracelet
suq	market
tahmiyah	annealing
tamimah diniyyah	religious amulet
taqleed	false or imitation (gem)
tarq	hammering
Tibi	Tibetan (adj)
Turki	Turkish (adj)
ud	stringed instrument
umla	coins
'uwayneh	blue beads
wasat	ring for the third finger
Yamani	Yemeni (adj)
zakhrafa	embossing
zand (pl. zunud)	armlet
zarir	bells
zirr (pl. azrar)	button
zujaj	glass

GLOSSARY OF TECHNICAL TERMS

A Jour   Open like lace.

Amulet   Object worn to protect the wearer against evil, commonly called a charm.

Annealing   Softening of metal by alternately heating and cooling to remove brittleness and make it malleable for working.

Assay   The testing of metals to ensure that they are of standard fineness.

Baroque pearl   A pearl of irregular shape.

Bezel   The upper part of a finger-ring, usually holding a stone.

Cabochon   Gemstone polished without facets, giving a domed appearance.

Cameo   Shell or stone carved with a design in relief (opposite of intaglio).

Casting   Shaping of piece of metal by melting and pouring into a mould.

Ceramic   Pottery made from clay, fired in a kiln, and often glazed.

Champlévé   Recesses carved out of metal which are then filled with enamel.

Chasing   A decorative technique in which the design is traced out on metal by blows of a punch from the front. There are two types of chasing: flat and with repoussé.

Cire Perdue   The method of casting where the wax model is set in packed sand. The molten metal is poured into the mould replacing the wax which melts away. [Lost wax process].

Cloisonné   Narrow strips of metal bent to form cells, soldered to a solid base and then filled with enamel.

Collet   The encompassing band or ringed flange forming setting or socket for a stone; often filed partially away to make claws.

Draw-plate   A piece of hard metal with holes of varying size through which wire can be tugged; by using successively smaller holes, the wire eventually reaches the required even gauge.

Electrum   The natural alloy of gold and silver.

Embossing   Similar to repousse. A process of raising a domed design on the front of the metal by beating it with punches and a hammer from behind.

Engraving   Technique for cutting patterns in a surface with a sharp tool called a graver.

Facet   A plane surface on a gem which has been cut to reflect light.

Faience   Term conventionally used for ancient glazed composition with a quartz base. Also a term given to glazed earthenware.

Filigree   Ornamental wire-work formed into delicate tracery sometimes soldered to a metal background but occasionally left as openwork.

Finial   Topmost capping of pinnacle, or capping, eg: on end of horseshoe bracelet.

Fusing   A technique for cleanly joining two metal objects together by melting with intense heat, using copper carbonate as a flux.

Gem   An object fashioned from a gemstone.

Gemstone   Treasured mineral found in the earth, and including the organic compound, amber, and non-minerals eg coral, pearl, jet etc.

Glass   Non-crystalline solid substance made by fusing sand with soda or potash, or both; usually with other ingredients.

Granulation   Minute balls or grains of metal fused to a flat metal surface to produce raised surface decoration.

Hammering   Term applied to the process of hammering annealed metal into flat sheets before cutting and shaping.

Intaglio   An engraved stone, the design being sunk into its surface – a carved design hollowed out, the opposite to cameo in which the background is carved away.

Jewel   Ornament worn for personal adornment usually containing stones.

Lapidary   One who cuts all precious gemstones, excluding diamonds.

Mandrel   A metal rod round which a ribbon of thin metal is wound to create hollow wire; or rod around which metal is forged or shaped.

Mineral   Any compound or element occurring naturally as a product of inorganic processes.

Niello   A composition of sulphur, silver and other metals used like enamel; of a metallic black appearance.

Non-mineral   Organic fossils but including pearls, coral jet etc.

Opus interassile   A method of piercing an open pattern in metal with a chisel not a saw.

Paste   Glass used to imitate precious stones.

Repousse   Decorative technique for working sheet metal in which the design is hammered out from behind with punches to raise a pattern which stands out in relief on the front.

Shank   The hoop of a finger-ring.

Shot   Minute grains of metal achieved by heating a metal fragment to melting point when it is rolled into perfectly spherical droplets.

Shoulder   Plain or decorated piece of metal attached to shank and bezel of a finger ring

Soldering   A method for assembling the basic parts of a piece of jewellery. It employs a similar metal to the pieces to be joined but one which is alloyed to a lower melting point than the ornament. A flux, or fusing agent, is used to wet the two surfaces to be joined and allow the molten solder to flow.

Spacer   A bead or bar pierced at intervals and threaded to ensure that multiple strands of beads and links remain correctly spaced in relation to each other.

Stone   Term applied to a gemstone, a gem and a jewel.

Talisman   Object worn to protect wearer from evil or bring him good fortune.

Terminal   A featured end of a bracelet, armlet or anklet and the end bead in a necklace.

Wrought Metal   Metal worked into shape by twisting or bending after being made malleable.

INDEX